Luminous Limericks

A collection of original limericks, written and illustrated by

Gregory Pastoll

This limerick writer, I'm told
Didn't like many tame ones of old.
So he set out to write
Some more that weren't trite,
But brazen and brassy and bold.

Copyright and origination

The contents of this book, both text and illustrations, are entirely the work of the author, who retains the copyright in them.

© Gregory Pastoll 2021

This work was first published by Gregory Pastoll in 2021

Cover design and typesetting by Ross MacLennan

Cover artwork by Gregory Pastoll

ISBN 978-0-6484665-9-8 (paperback)

This book is available from online booksellers.

Recommendation

by

Ted Price, former Editor of the Taupo Times, New Zealand, and winner of the Pacific Area Newspaper Publishers' Association Journalism and Community Leadership awards.

Mark Twain said: '*Humanity has unquestionably one really effective weapon—laughter. … Against the assault of laughter nothing can stand.*'

After living through a 'year of interesting times', laughter surely remains the best medicine, and we all need a gigantic dose. Here it is folks, prescribed by our good doctor Gregory Pastoll. Luminous Limericks is a quick fix for the world's woes.

This is a delightfully presented and timely piece. Keep one handy to combat the afflictions of boredom and despair.

And don't forget your friends and enemies: I recommend this cure to all.

Acknowledgements

The continuing support and understanding shown me by my wife Lindsay, especially when I spend long periods of time tucked away in my study, working away at something that might one day possibly be useful.

The occasional indications of approval from my family and friends when I have shown them particular limericks. Encouraging feedback is always welcome to any author.

Mr Edward Lear (1812 - 1888), bless his dear departed cotton socks, for inspiring me to start off on this path of distraction.

Preface

All limericks are written for the purpose of amusement.

A limerick is probably the shortest form of a short story that there is. Each one covers in its brief five lines something fictional that we can all relate to, such as a supposed event, or the foibles of some type of character.

As a recognised form of rhyming verse, the limerick has been around since at least the time of Shakespeare, and probably long before that.

The first collection of limericks to be published was Edward Lear's 'Book of Nonsense', that came out in 1846. My family had a later edition of this book. For me, as a child, Lear's book was a blast. Since those days, I have encountered many limericks written by others, many of them more venturesome and punchy than those of good Mr Lear.

Interestingly, Lear did not use the word 'limerick' to describe his verse. He just called them nonsense rhymes.

The word 'nonsense' is pivotal when it comes to limericks. Most limericks are nonsensical in that they take your mind on a flight of imagination. They reflect our world to us in an oblique way, through exaggeration and improbable happenings, involving characters who lampoon the sorts of people we know (including ourselves) and the sorts of ways that they react to events.

It is hard to think of limericks as poetry. For me, the difference is: whereas a poem is supposed to make the reader *feel*, a successful limerick ought to make you *laugh*, and all the better if it makes you *think*, as well.

I have written the limericks in this book in short bursts of activity spaced over several years, in between other projects. I write them because I enjoy reading other people's good limericks.

What makes a good limerick, as opposed to a bad one? Discipline, definitely. It has to rhyme properly (near-rhymes are completely infra dig) and it has to scan properly. It has to make sense, and has to have punch.

The character of a given limerick might be droll, funny, philosophical, irreverent, wise, tongue-in-cheek, bawdy, or several of these at once.

There is a class of limerick that people love to recite clandestinely and snigger about, mainly for the reason that it is not deemed 'proper' to talk about such things in the open, or to use the taboo words with which they abound. This class of limerick deals mainly with subjects that include sexually excessive exploits and extremely impossible events, such as explosions that result in sensitive body parts being found on adjacent continents.

For the open-minded, laughing at limericks of this sort is a wonderful way of letting off steam. I have no idea what the the closed-minded do to amuse themselves. However, for the sake of not wanting to contribute too much to the collapse of civilisation, I am omitting from the present collection limericks of this type.

The limericks you will find here tell stories about many different aspects of life. Some might deal with professors, musicians, artists, plumbers or daredevils, but some are there purely to make light of the delightful idiocies found in the English language.

I don't know if people write limericks in any language besides English. It must be possible, of course, but English provides particularly large scope for playing on words.

The limericks in this collection are grouped into sets, according to themes. These sets are not watertight, because it is often hard to allocate any one limerick to only one particular category.

This collection does not include any limericks that poke fun at real people in public life. Nor does it touch on the topics of politics or religion. This is not to say that these realms of endeavour are without amusing, ridiculous, or absurd features, worthy of lampooning. However, it is not this writer's aim to criticise or moralise or stir up hornet's nests of indignation.

A point about a feature common to many limericks: It is usual, though not compulsory, for a limerick to invoke the name of a person or place. For example, a limerick might start off with: 'There was a young fellow called Jones…'

There is a very practical reason for this. It is often hard to find three ordinary words that rhyme for the endings of lines 1, 2 and 5. So we frequently need some proper nouns to fulfil that task. If we make use of your name or the name of your town or country, it is for literary convenience, and not because we want to insult you. In fact, it is not our aim to insult anyone. These limericks are written in the spirit of fond and sympathetic amusement for the human foibles that we are all prone to.

So, what do you do with a limerick? You simply read it for fun, like you might read a comic… or an encyclopaedia. A good limerick will fulfil some of the functions of both.

Jump in.

Contents

Recommendation
Acknowledgements
Preface

The limericks are grouped in sets according to themes. Sets 4 and 10 do not have specific themes, and for various reasons, are not illustrated. All the other sets are illustrated.

1. People Doing Silly Things	1
2. The Consequences of Unfortunate Circumstances	38
3. Health Issues	68
4. No Pictures, no Pictures!	75
5. Playing with words	80
6. So-called Intelligentsia	91
7. Musical Maladies	99
8. A Tinge of Romance	114
9. Artistic Anomalies	127
10. More Without Pictures	133
11. Parenting and Children	138
12. Sporting Shenanigans	155
13. Pure Fantasy	169
14. Secrets from History	180
15. Clothing Conundrums	185
Appendix: Suggestions for writing your own limericks	207
About the Author	214
Extracts from other published rhyming stories by this author	216

People doing silly things

A crafty old fellow from Cork
Took to taking a sponge for a walk.
It wasn't for petting:
He did it for getting
His taciturn neighbours to talk.

There was an old German called Weitz
Who took getting drunk to new heights:
　　With schnapps as his power
　　He climbed up a tower
And clung there for three solid nights.

A canoeist with minimal guile
Went over some falls on the Nile.
That was not his intention:
But here, we must mention:
Getting back was a bit of a trial.

For a dare, a young fellow called Eric
Once scoffed a whole jar of turmeric:
    His hair went erect,
    And the anal effect
Was rapid and quite atmospheric.

A skate-boarding scumbag from Skerry
Tried skating the length of a ferry.
He hopped on the rail,
But plunged, with a wail:
A sight most deliciously merry.

A London commuter called Ollie
Committed the ultimate folly
By boarding his train
With a tie that was plain
And a floral design on his brolly.

A gullible guy from Gonubie
Once bought what he thought was a ruby.
His wife, ever bright,
Said: 'Ooh, Turkish Delight!
How generous, darling, can you be!'

There was an old man in a chair
Who didn't have very much hair.
His barber said: 'Mate,
If there's one thing I hate,
It's cutting what isn't quite there!

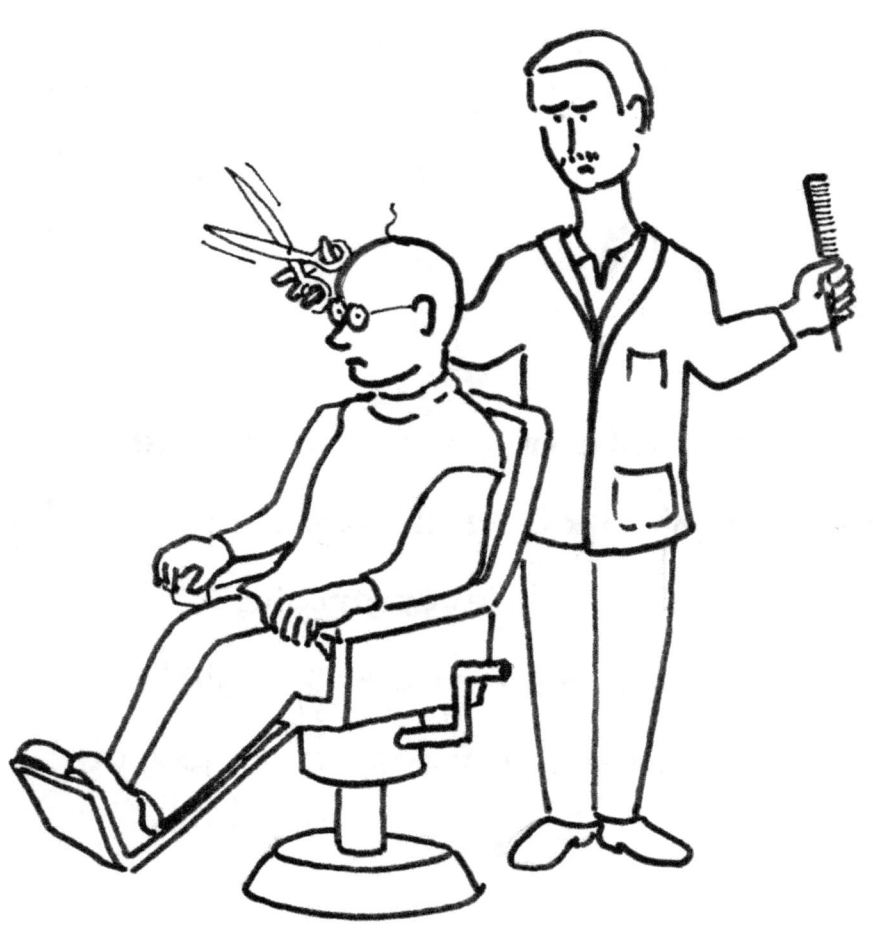

A builder called Bill was delighted
To hear that his son had been knighted:
He went to the palace
But called the Queen 'Alice':
A wrong that has never been righted.

A dodgy young dude who was fickle
Was flippantly flipping a nickel,
To decide who to knife:
a. His girl b. His wife,
But it landed on edge. What a pickle!

There was an old man of Tobruk
Who told everyone he could cook,
But he was a liar:
What came off the fire
For fossilised turds were mistook.

A macho mechanic called Jason
Once cleaned off some gears in his basin.
His wife said: 'Enough!
You can pack up your stuff!
That basin and you need replacin'!'

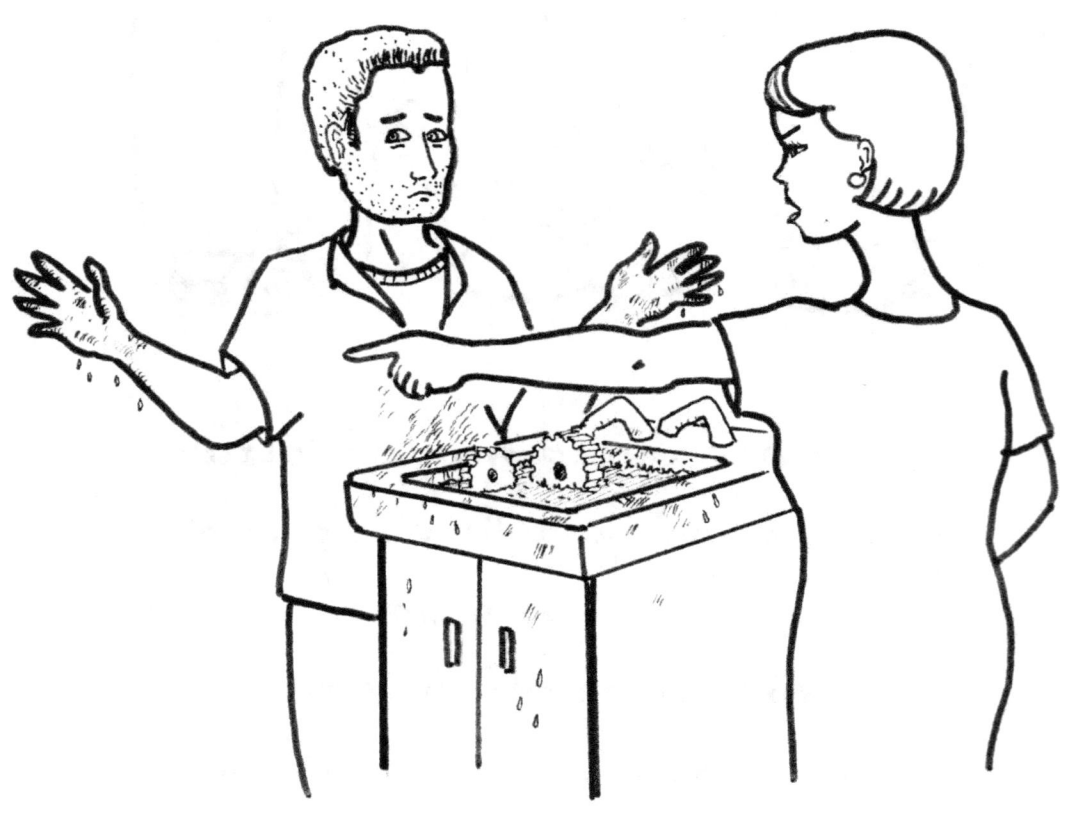

A fussy young fellow from Kush,
Once ate a whole mulberry bush.
He savoured the wood,
And the leaves tasted good,
But the fruit he declined: it was mush.

There was an old man of Toulouse
Who was thoroughly given to booze:
 He was given quite hard,
 Being thrown in the yard,
And after him sailed his shoes.

Some hillbillies built a big raft
Made of barrels, all tied to a shaft.
When it went in the drink,
And proceeded to sink:
They plinked on their banjos, and laughed.

A greedy old gourmand called Bryce,
Was once offered lipstick on rice.
He said: 'I should think
That my poo will be pink,
But, damn it all, let's have a slice!'

A pimply young man from Hafeez
Absent-mindedly started to squeeze.
At the sight of the pus,
All the folks on the bus
Found their heads fast approaching their knees.

To a sceptical man of Navarre,
A psychic declared: 'You'll go far!'
Perhaps she was right:
For the very same night,
He set off for Rome in his car.

An obedient laddie from Riding
Was giving his old man a hiding.
His father yelled: 'More!
It is not even sore!':
A very strange reason for chiding.

A globetrotting lady called Julia
Went to see the strange folks of Bengoolia.
But when she got there,
To her shock and despair,
Those people thought she was peculiar.

'It is time I should buy a new scooter,'
Said a fellow who rode around Kuta.
   There was nothing amiss
   With the old one, get this:
But the volume was down on the hooter.

There was a young Aussie called Midge
Who was learning to play on the didge.
His teacher said: 'Bro,
Play it cool when you blow,'
So Midge put his didge in the fridge.

An elegant lady from Deal
Once balanced herself on a wheel.
She walked it downtown
And she wouldn't get down,
Despite a big public appeal.

A daredevil dude known as Odo
Once went to the isle of Komodo.
He fancied a ride
On a dragon. He tried,
But ended up just like the dodo.

A salty old seaman from Hayle
Arrived at the docks on a whale.
When they said: 'What a skill!'
He replied: 'As you will,
But I'm thinking of adding a sail.'

The inventions of Marvin Binotti
Were really quite pointless and dotty.
For instance, a scope
On the end of a rope
To measure the depth of a potty.

An aircraft designer called Lane
Designed a submersible plane.
A man from the press
Said: 'It looks good, I guess,
But, can it take off in the rain?'

A new-age disciple called Gwen
Would drift off while practising Zen:
  Which she was inclining
  To doing while ironing,
No burning ambitions, but then...

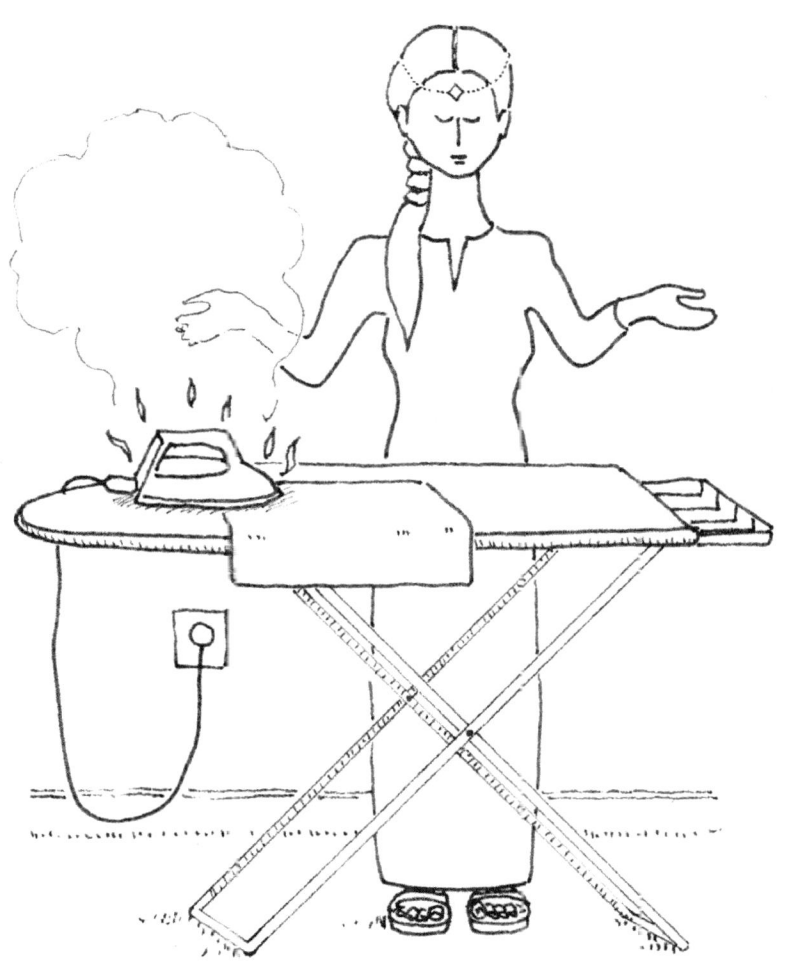

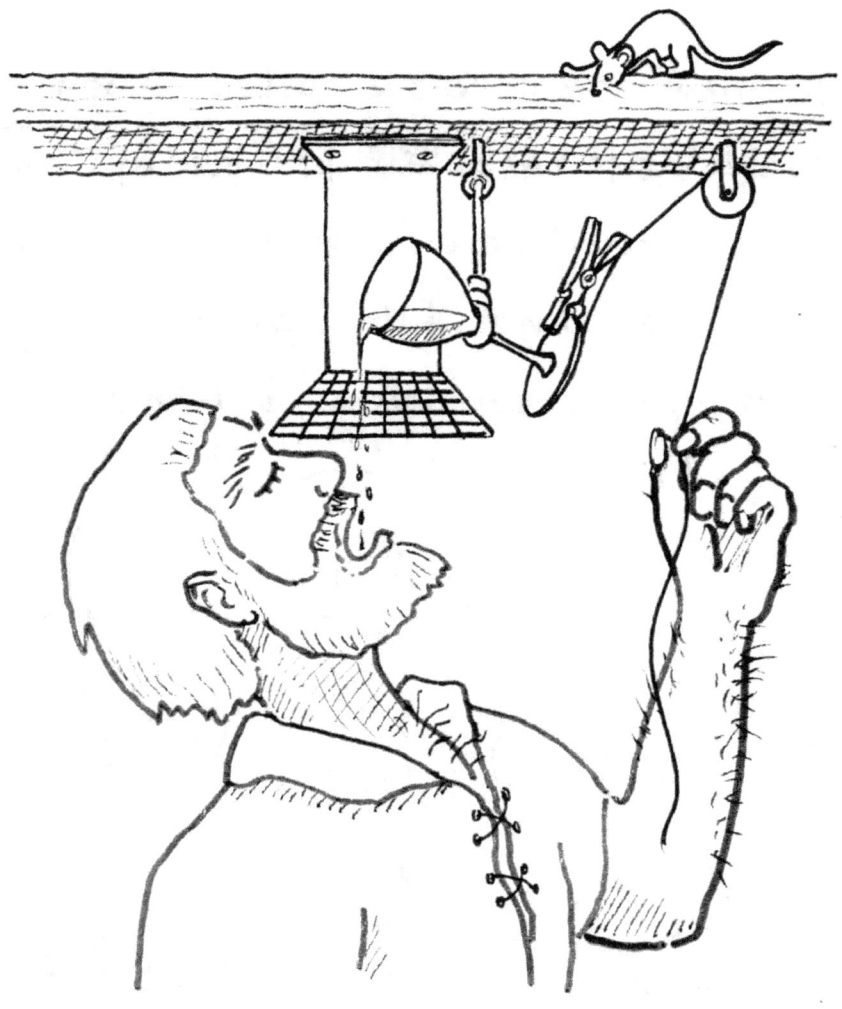

There was an old man of Madrid
Who always drank wine through a grid.
He feared he might gag
If some slug or some dag
Had somehow slipped under the lid.

A circus performer called Lars,
Determined to learn to eat glass,
Decided to practise
By chomping a cactus
To toughen his mouth and his arse.

A ten-year-old scholar called Hank
Drove up to his class in a tank,
Disdaining a car,
With a plastic cigar,
And four-star lapels, like a Yank.

There is an old Scot called McMartin
Whose lifestyle is thrifty and spartan:
But he's not as frugal
As Fergus McDougal,
Who 'can't afford' stripes on his tartan.

There was a young man on a mower
Whose girlfriend came through on the blower.
She informed him: 'No go,
You are miles too slow!'
So, he sped up, deciding to show her.

An old violin-maker called Brian
Constructed a 'cello from iron.
Was he keen to see tarnish,
Or was his new varnish
The stuff that he must have been high on?

Here's a thing which had never been tried:
A boy taught a hippo to ride.
It seems this depravity
Showed him that gravity
Never would thus be defied.

A silly young man from Vancouver
Tried cleaning his bum with a hoover,
He let out a curse
As it flipped to reverse:
You've never seen such a fast mover!

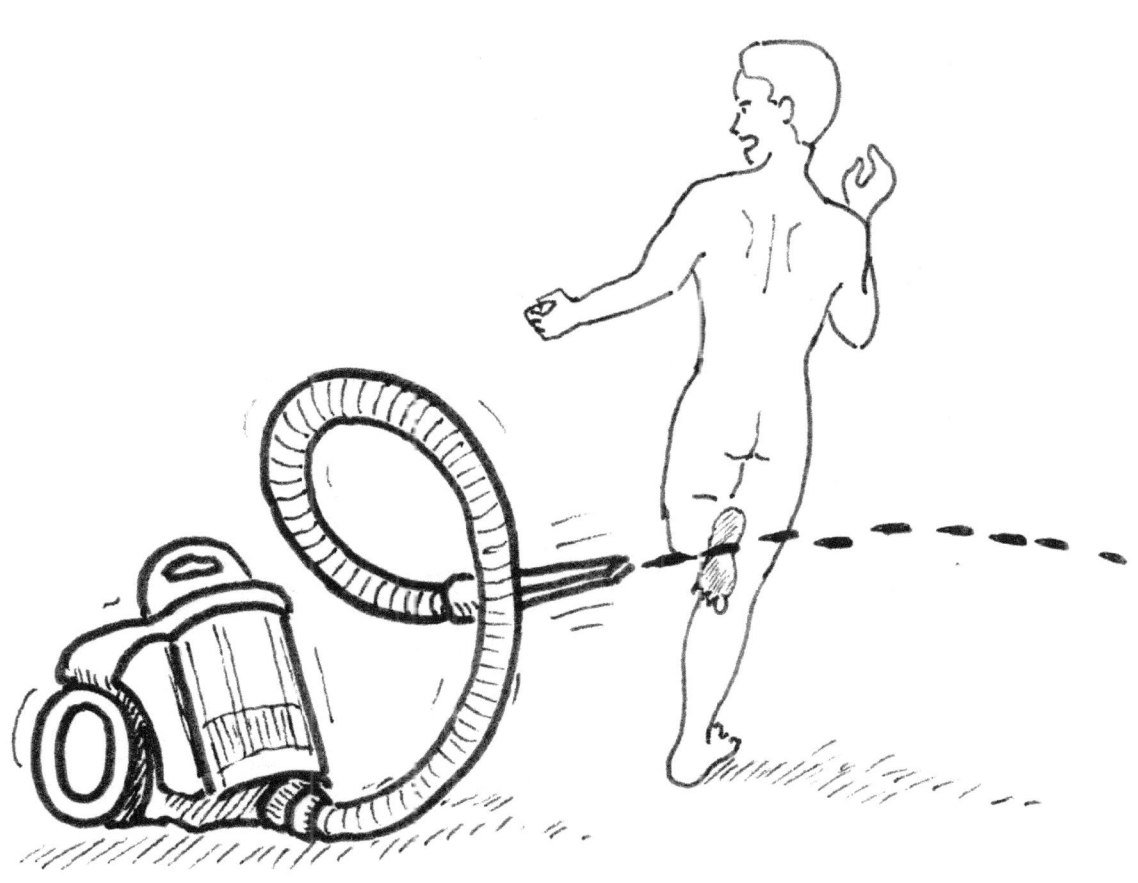

There was an old lady called Dockett,
Who kept a grenade in her pocket.
When Betty said: 'Gawd!
'Why the hell do that, Maud?'
She replied: 'Just in case, so don't knock it!'

There was an old codger called Cox
Who lived in a house full of clocks.
He thrived on the mix
Of the hundreds of ticks,
But hated the sound of the tocks.

The consequences of unfortunate circumstances

A very tall chap from Lahore
Hit his head on the frame of a door.
He uttered a sentence
Of utter repentance:
From then on, a turban he wore.

There was a young Welshman called Dai
Who saw a round disc in the sky:
He ran inside, screaming.
His dad said 'You're dreaming,
There ain't no such thing as a – Yiiii!'

A cheeky young man from Asuncion
Once gate-crashed the President's luncheon.
Soon back in the street,
He'd had nothing to eat,
Apart from some pieces of truncheon.

An apprentice magician called Sam
Got himself in a bit of a jam
When his boss disappeared
In a trick: It was weird,
Though it gave him no choice, but to scram.

A keen-eyed young man of Dubai
Was watching some eagles on high.
While craning his neck
He exclaimed: "What the heck!"
When a turd from a bird hit his eye.

A one-armed young airman called Ryder
Went up for a flip in a glider.
It started okay,
But it messed up his day
When his nose was attacked by a spider.

A capricious old woman from Parma
Once jumped on the back of a llama.
The llama got narked,
So he bucked and she carked,
Which I guess could be put down to karma.

A high-wire lady from Par
Once swung on a circus-type bar.
Her panty-band broke:
Though it wasn't a joke,
The applause was the loudest, by far.

There was an old man of Paloma
Whose chicken fell into a coma.
"What luck!" the man cried,
Then he plucked and he fried,
And he savoured the lovely aroma.

A tasteless performer named Bart
Was booed by the crowd, from the start.
They yelled: 'Sing in tune!'
So he flashed them his moon,
But his show was cut short by a dart.

There was a rich lady from Perth
Who had a spectacular girth.
They widened the doors
Of the sweet-shop, because
She guzzled for all she was worth.

An engineer's mate from Hibernia
Once measured a beam with a vernier.
He wasn't that bright,
But he managed alright,
Though doing it gave him a hernia.

A naughty young fellow from Como
Once swallowed a packet of Omo.
He bubbled for weeks
Out of both sets of cheeks:
It looked quite amazing in slo-mo.

If a train driver made a mistake
And he hit the emergency brake,
It could spoil your day
To the point where you may
Have to fish out an earful of cake.

A flyer was flying a flivver
That ditched in the Amazon river.
A pesky piranha
Attacked his banana,
So: one arrow less in his quiver.

Two hairy old men of Bavaria:
I don't know which one was the scarier:
They jumped in a pool
Where the crocodiles drool,
And the beasts all emerged in hysteria.

An emerald miner in China
Discovered a truly big shiner.
Do you think it weird
That the man disappeared,
And his boss bought a new ocean liner?

At one eating contest, when Mabel,
Who started as thin as a cable,
Began to partake
Of her seventeenth cake,
The watchers dived under the table.

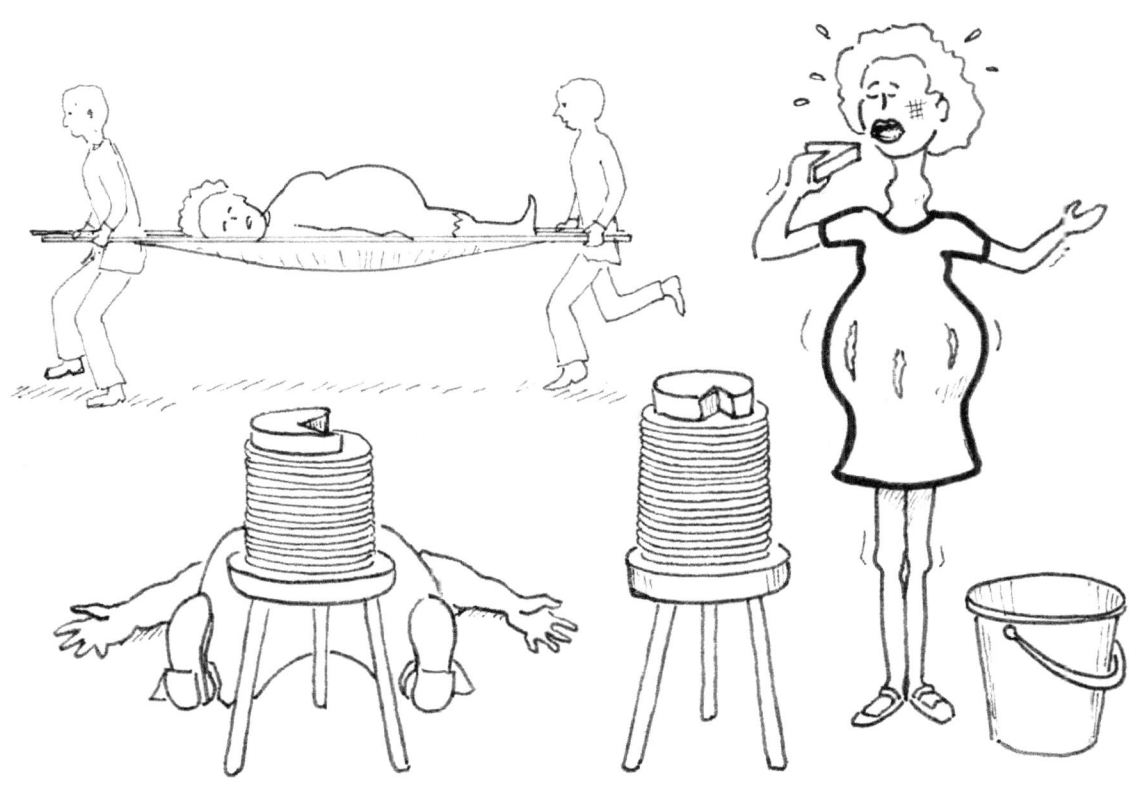

When Oliver fell down the steps, he
Was thought to have had epilepsy,
But it soon came to light:
At the top of the flight
He had snorted a bottle of Pepsi.

A lady exclaimed in alarm:
'My hairdo resembles a palm!'
'Well, then that equates:
You'll get plenty of dates!'
Said her stylist, just oozing with charm.

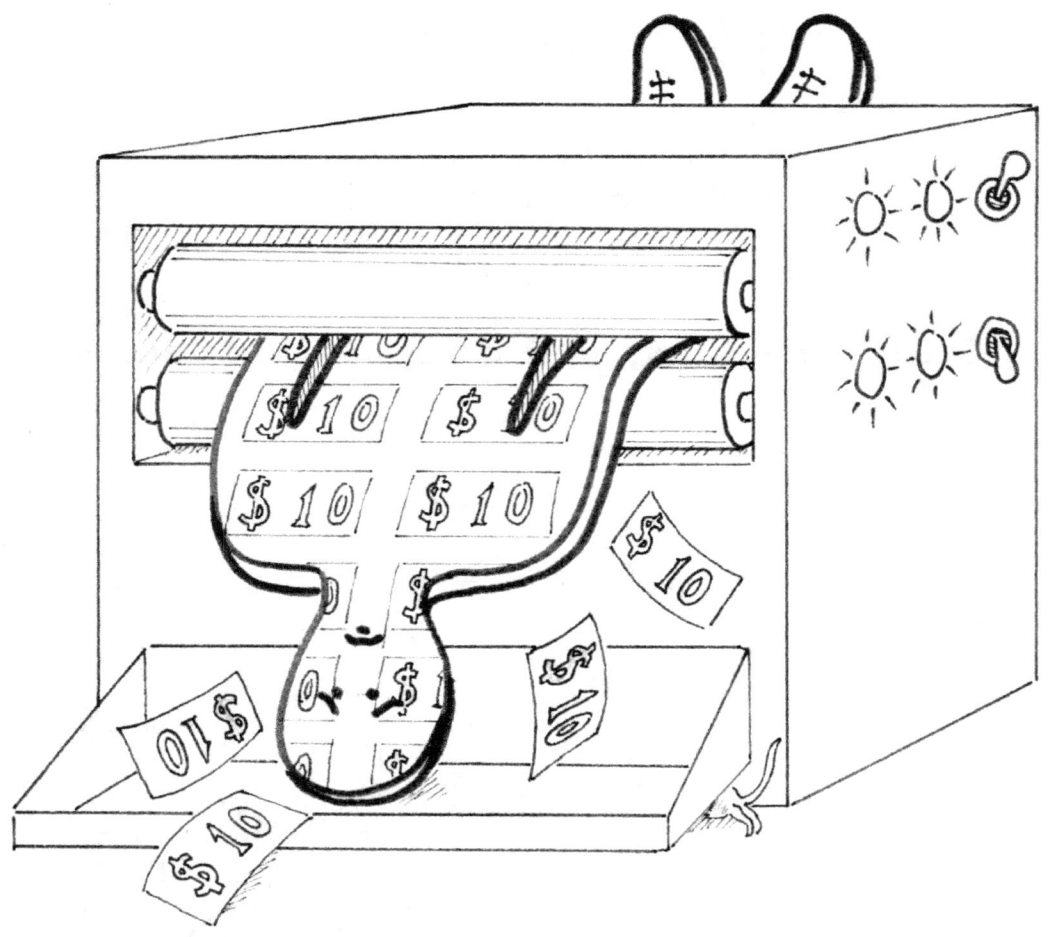

A scheming old forger called Nash
Once needed some cash in a flash:
In his haste and duress,
He got pulled through his press,
Coming out in a ten-dollar rash.

A pub-crawling pundit called Jack
Once tripped on a railway track.
He lay on the sleepers
And mumbled: 'Oh, Jeepers,
Zhish bed's not sho good for me back!'

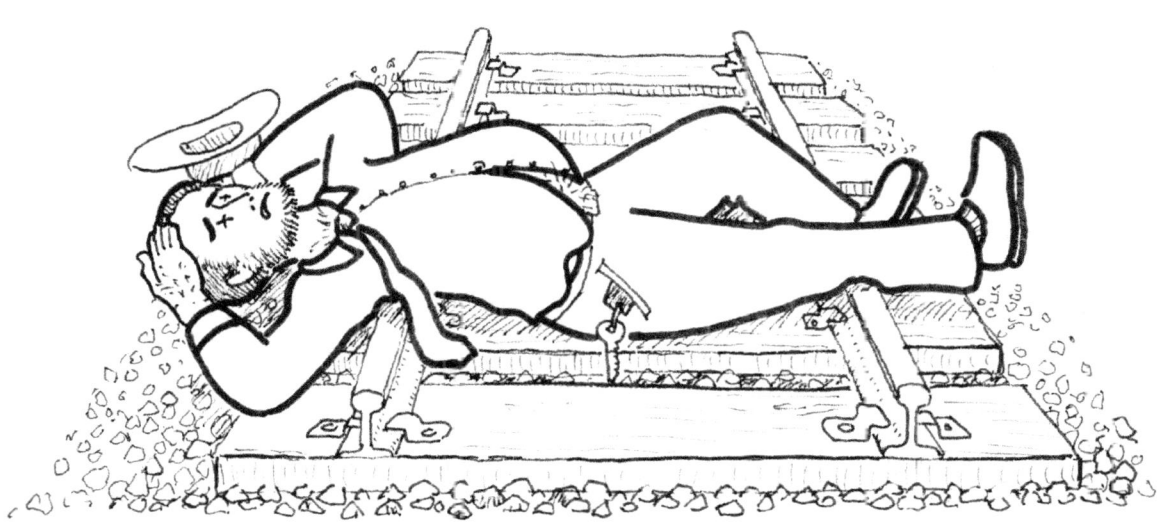

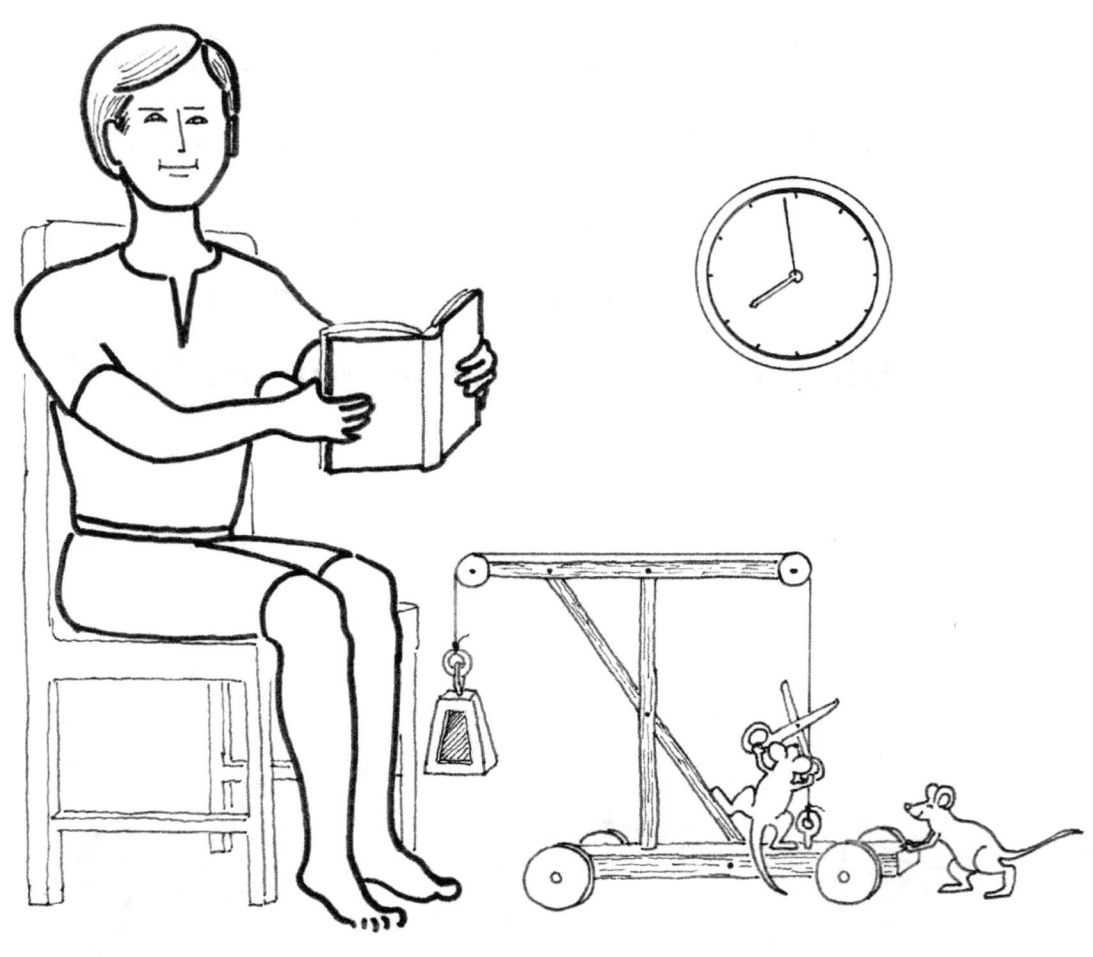

Phineas Phillip McPherson
Was really a very nice person.
But, if you dropped a weight
On his toe, after eight,
His placid demeanour would worsen.

There was an old maid of Cadiz,
Who got herself all in a tizz,
She found that some ants
Had invaded her pants,
And her fuzz was beginning to fizz.

I knew an old joker, out West,
Who shot up my vest, for a jest.
My reaction? Of course,
I just sold off his horse.
But, neither has ever confessed.

There was a young man of Kazoo
Who stifled a cow in mid-moo.
He got his desserts
'Cos the cow had the squirts
And made a fine mess of his shoe.

Giuseppe received a rude letter
Informing him he was a debtor.
The lawyer who sent it
Soon came to repent it:
Giuseppe replied by Beretta.

An eager young man with a noose,
Decided to lasso a moose.
That wasn't so wise:
He developed black eyes,
And a couple of molars came loose.

An author said: "Look, mama, look!
The publisher's published my book!'
'No surprise,' declared she,
He's your papa, you see:
To publish mine, that's what it took!'

A cautious young fellow called Crumb
Once ate seven-eighths of a plum.
He left all the rest
To the resident pest,
With a view to preserving his bum.

Health Issues

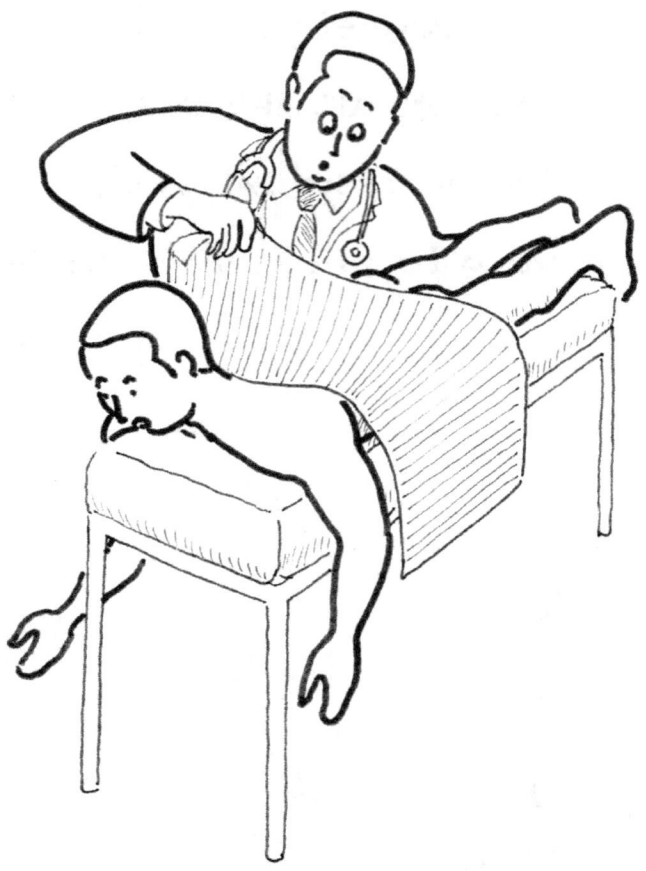

There was a young man of Elysium
Who liked to eat bowls of magnesium.
His doctor said: 'Mate,
Carry on at this rate,
And your arsehole will be a trapezium!'

There was a young fellow from Düssel,
Whose toothbrush had only one bristle.
　　His dentist said: 'Sherbert!
　　That won't cut it, Herbert,
You're better off using a thistle!'

Every day, a young boy in Tasmania
Showed signs of becoming much brainer.
His doctor surmised:
'I am hardly surprised,
This chap has a spare set of crania!'

A scruffy old man from the Grange
Presented with four types of mange.
One peep at this yob,
And his doc quit the job,
Convinced it was time for a change.

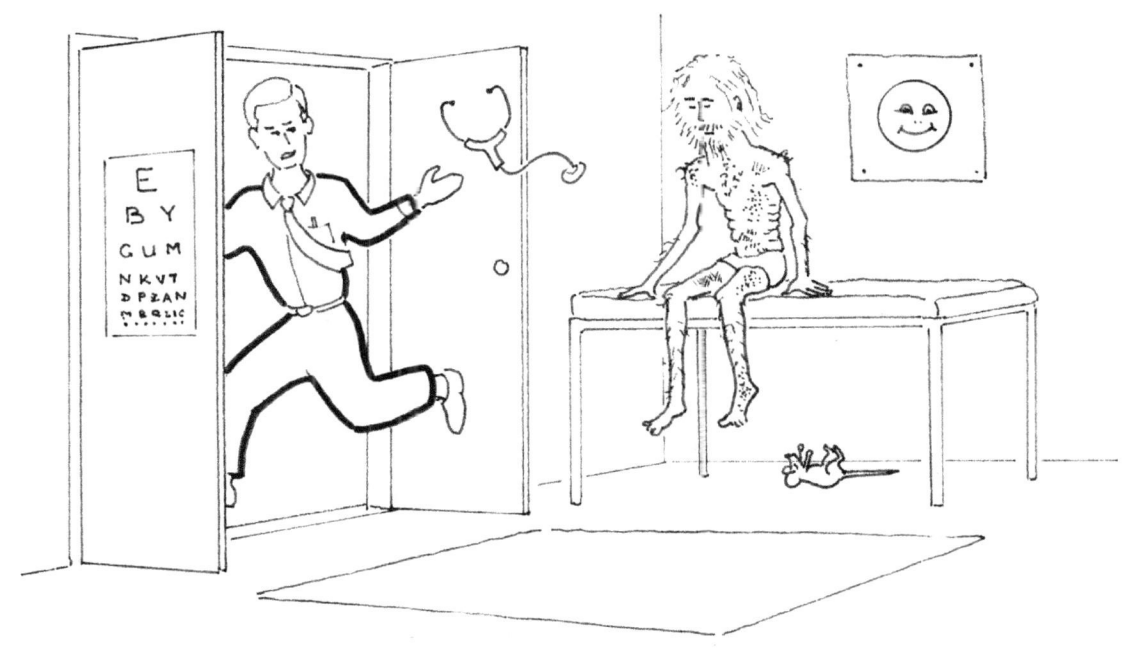

A peculiar man from Electum,
Once claimed to have more than one rectum.
His doctor said: 'Gosh!
For a whole heap of dosh,
I will see if my scope can detect 'em!'

There was an old man in a hut
Who liked keeping everything shut.
He lost vital signs
In the airless confines,
And soon went the way of King Tut.

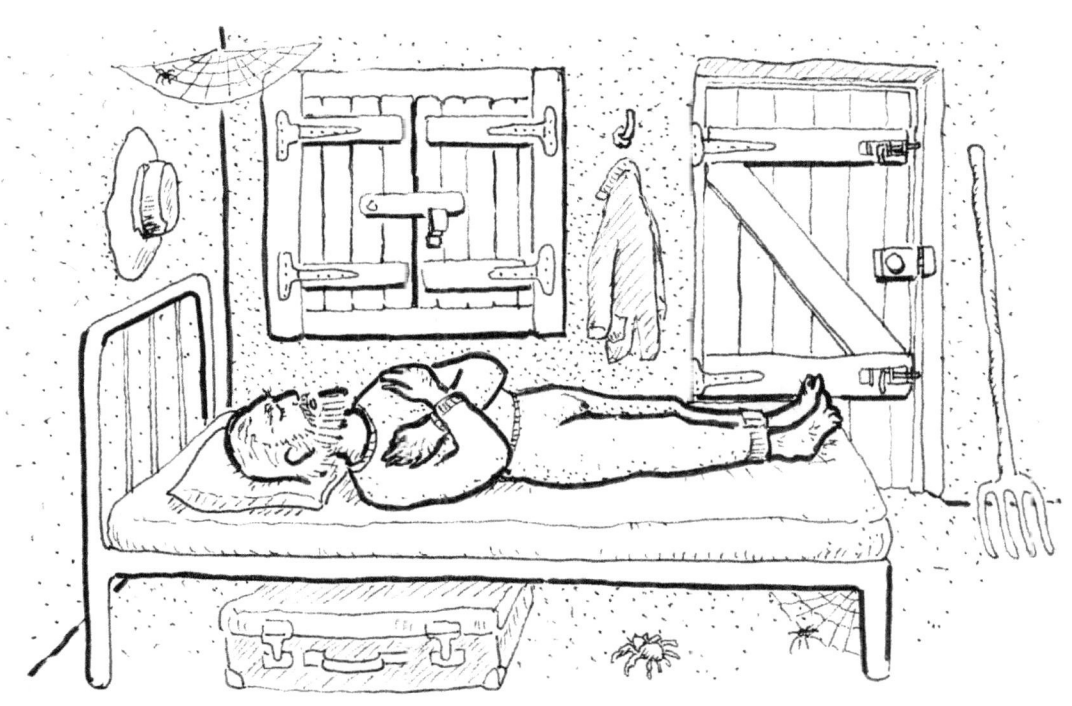

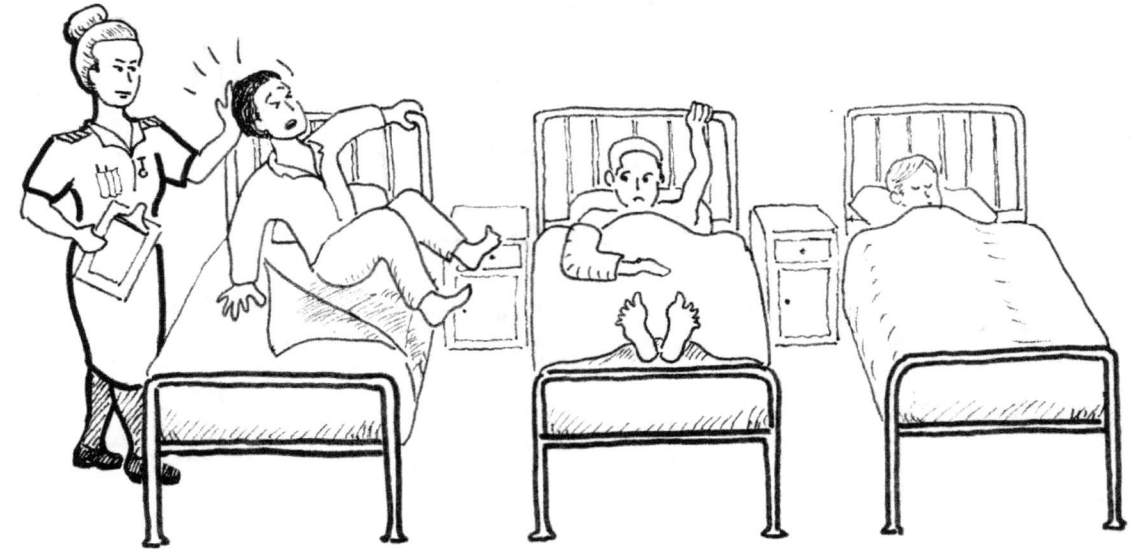

A certain old matron from Bickley
Would slap everyone who was sickly.
They fled from their beds,
With a sting in their heads,
Taking pains to recover quite quickly.

No pictures, no pictures!

This section contains limericks that would be difficult to illustrate, for various reasons that will become apparent.

A gushing young lady from Dunning
Declared everything to be 'stunning!':
 This lass was so stunned
 That they set up a fund
To keep her adrenalin running.

A man from a circus in Dee
Once went on a juggling spree:
 He'll end up in Hades
 For juggling three ladies,
And catching them all before tea.

An old politician called James
Was mightily fond of the dames:
He was up to his tricks
When they caught him with six,
But he wouldn't divulge any names.

There was a young fellow from Henshil
Whose uncle was most influential:
He got him a seat
In the Lords, which was neat,
But a very large bribe was essential.

You see that young man there, Carruthers?
We're told he's the third of three brothers.
His father was crowned,
And has gotten around,
So the talk is: there may well be others.

The mayor of Morton-on-Tweedie
Was quietly cunning and greedy.
　　Some dealings with land
　　Had occurred underhand:
He prospered, but not so the needy.

A bloke was caught driving while nude.
The officer said: "I'm no prude,
　　Lady, get off his lap,
　　Or I'm charging this chap
With driving while not in the mood.

A headstrong young fellow called Rice
Just didn't like taking advice:
　　He married at ten,
　　And at thirteen, again,
Both chosen by rolling the dice.

A taciturn fellow from Russia
Went out with a girl who's a gusher.
When they said: 'That's absurd!
Did you get in one word?'
He replied with a nod to the crusher.

We had an old teacher: at break
He had something besides tea and cake.
It came from a packet
Tucked into his jacket,
And caused him to shine and to shake.

Once, after a minor transgression,
A girl was sent off to confession.
But she felt kind of nice
When she spoke of her vice,
And she let it become her profession.

Two figurines made out of wax
Decided to live to the max:
They climbed on the roof
For a bit of a goof,
But melted, and fell through the cracks.

Just Playing with Words

A quokka, a quoll and a quenda,
Had been on a bit of a bender.
They argued the toss
About who was the boss,
And which one was which, and what gender.

A leading exponent of leading
Was reading a reading at Reading.
By chance this good sage
Skipped the whole of one page,
So no-one knew where he was heading.

I phought for a pharaoh called Ptolemy
Who yelled to his soldiers to "pfollow me!"
But, just as I feared,
All the Hittites appeared,
And I wished that the desert would pswallow me.

A very young Brit in Bordeaux
Complained that she hadn't seen sneaux.
Her mother said: "Esther,
We're miles from Chester,
So, can it and geaux with the fleaux.

A really rich rancher called Blanche
Had lunch on a launch on her ranch,
But the launch did a lurch
When it beached on a birch,
And she launched all her lunch on a branch.

A thieving young thug called Theroux
Tried to sneak through the bars of a zoo:
But, he'd eaten that night,
And the gap was too tight,
So Theroux had not thought the thing through.

A grumpy old man of Versailles
Was pestered to hell by a fly.
He yelled: That's enough!
I don't give a stough!
"Today is the day that you dailles!"

A bright little girl called Jemima
Once thought of becoming a rhymer.
But she gave up this plan
When amusing her gran
By trying to rhyme 'limber' with 'climber'.

There was a young man of Pompeii
Who was nothing, if not very gay:
He used to parade
In an outfit of jade,
But Vesuvius blew him away.

Two termites called Trevor and Titus
Developed severe termititus:
According to Trevor,
'It happens whenever
We argue about Heraclitus'.

A very smart lady called Jen
Invented the ultimate pen.
It could do so much more
Than the version before,
Which became the penultimate then.

So-called Intelligentsia

A philatelist man of good breeding
Fell asleep in his chair after reading.
He woke in a sweat
With his strongest curse yet,
Having dreamt that his stamps were stampeding.

There once was a student of thought,
Who knew everything he'd been taught.
But he didn't own
Any thoughts of his own,
Which is sad: you'd have thought that he ought.

A buck-toothed professor called Park
Announced a snap test on the quark.
　They felt unprepared,
　Till one joker declared:
'His bite is much worse than his mark!'

A professor of fizzy-pop fluxion
Once made a fantastic deduction:
He'd studied a straw
For a decade or more,
Concluding: what drove it was suction.

A man who was mad about science
Once built a robotic appliance.
It went for his throat,
And the silly old goat
Got throttled while humming defiance.

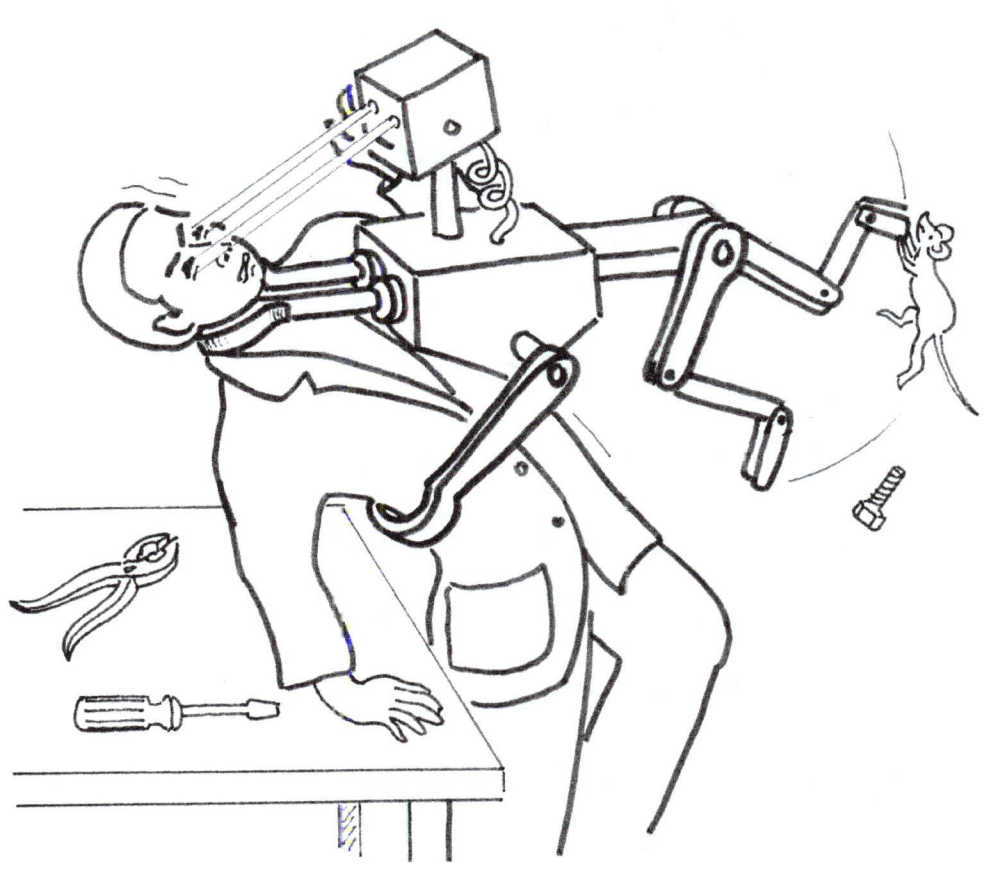

Greg Pastoll

While munching a mulberry muffin,
A scholar was studying a puffin.
The puffin said 'Boo!
I am studying you too!'
Boy, if that didn't kill, it would toughen.

I once knew a student at college:
Though bright and quite brimful of knowledge,
And had never been canned,
He could not understand
Why someone would want to eat porridge.

A feminist said 'You're a floozy:
'I do not approve of you, Susie!'
'Too bad, you're just jealous!
Who'd look at you? Tell us!
But, I can afford to be choosy!'

Musical Maladies

A certain young lady, in France,
Once asked her small brother to dance.
He told her, in French,
As he clung to his bench:
'Marie, you have bugger-all chance!'

A musical maestro called Matt,
Was so fond of the key of e-flat
He could fart in that pitch
With a sound deep and rich:
The vibrato was done with his hat.

A tone-deaf ex-hippie, called Bailey
Got hold of an old ukulele.
He had no idea
What affront to the ear
He caused, but he plinked on it, gaily.

Young Strauss had sat down to compose,
When his quill-feather tickled his nose.
He started to sneeze:
Repetitions of threes:
Which is how the waltz tempo arose.

A coloratura called Dee
Could sing forty notes above C:
The sound of her trilling
Was equally thrilling
As drilling a hole in your knee.

A wayward old pianist called Coates
Couldn't help playing too many notes:
When remanded he'd say
He got 'carried away',
Which did not only happen in quotes.

A cobra once said to a mamba:
'Come join me in dancing a rumba!'
'We can dance intertwined!'
But the mamba declined,
Having heard about cobras. Caramba!

A rock and a roll were debating
Why dances they knew were frustrating.
Said the rock to the roll:
'What they lack, on the whole,
Is something to get you gyrating.'

The triangle player was late
So a 'cellist stood in for his mate.
He used a tomato
To ting with vibrato
Which made the conductor deflate.

A metronome-maker called Mike
Added all sorts of spokes to his bike
To clack out a ditty.
He rode round the city,
Playing country and classics alike.

A marching band drummer called Nick
Lost hold of the end of one stick:
It bounced up his nose:
For a moment he froze,
Then he sneezed, and five people were sick.

Greg Pastoll

While dancing a dainty fandango,
A couple tripped over a mango.
With impressive gymnastic,
They stayed up: fantastic,
Inventing what's known as the tango.

I once had a friendly flamingo
That went by the nickname of 'Ringo'.
'Is he good on the drums?'
Sniggered one of my chums.
'Not really. My drummer's a dingo.'

Next door to me once lived a dude
Whose guitar-playing level was crude:
He knew only one chord
Which he clearly adored
But ignored the effect on my mood.

Forget the old staid Bossa Nova,
There's a dance called the Spinning Pavlova:
    You gobble some jelly
    And wobble your belly
While twirling, and spray it all over.

A Tinge of Romance

There was a young nun in a priory
Whose protests were heartfelt and fiery
When implored to explain
Why a fellow called Wayne
Still featured so much in her diary.

A gorgeous young lady in red
Once climbed into somebody's bed.
He woke up, amazed,
Gasping: 'Heaven be praised!'
But, she saw where she was, and she fled.

The wife of a tycoon called Jones
Had fifty erogenous zones.
They ranged from Gibraltar,
Majorca to Malta:
He found out about this from drones.

While quite unaware of his peril
Young Errol took kindly to Beryl:
　He tried to say 'Hi',
　But she spat in his eye:
Revealing that Beryl was feral.

There was a young lady called Hackett
Who possessed an electrified jacket.
If you pressed button one
She would light up with fun,
If your hand went near two, she would smack it!

If you lived in time of King Cyrus,
You would write to your girl on papyrus.
By the time her reply
Made it back to your eye,
You were old and no longer desirous.

Greg Pastoll

A crewman in space, in a shuttle
Said something that wasn't so subtle.
The space-girl in question
Disdained his suggestion
And gave him a cosmic rebuttal.

A young man went into a sauna
And picked up a strange type of fauna
That caused a red rash.
He went weak, in a flash:
Yep: the name of this creature was Shauna.

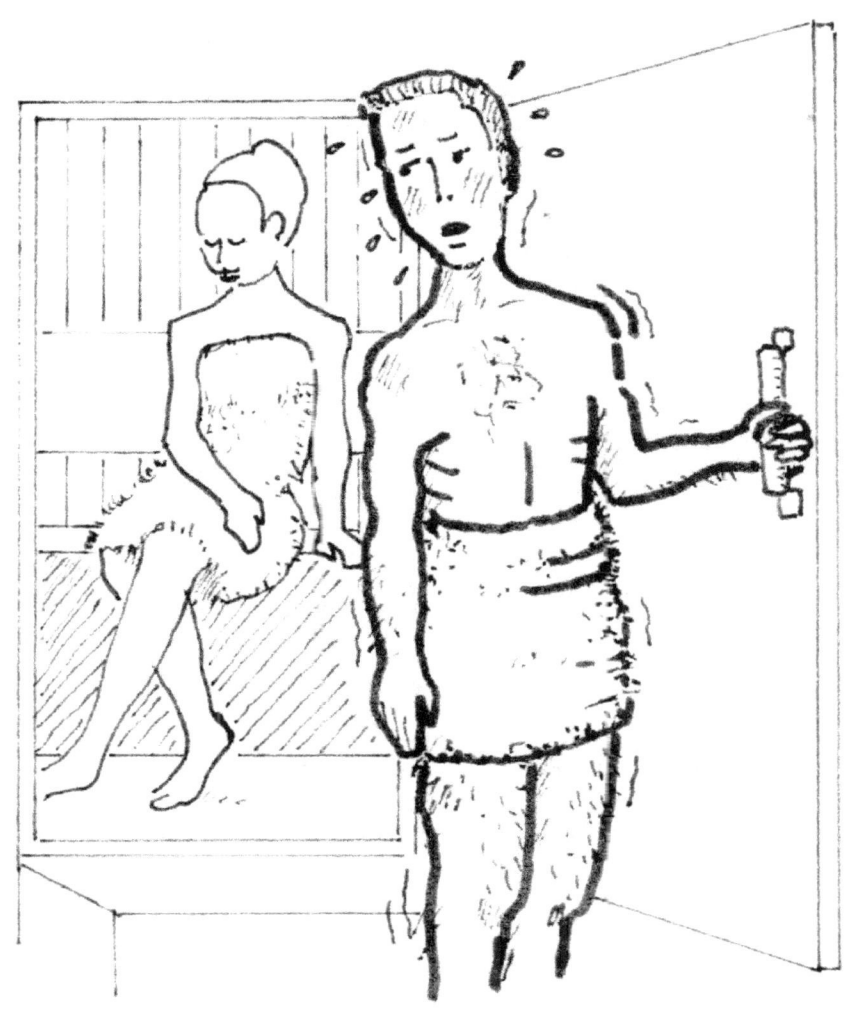

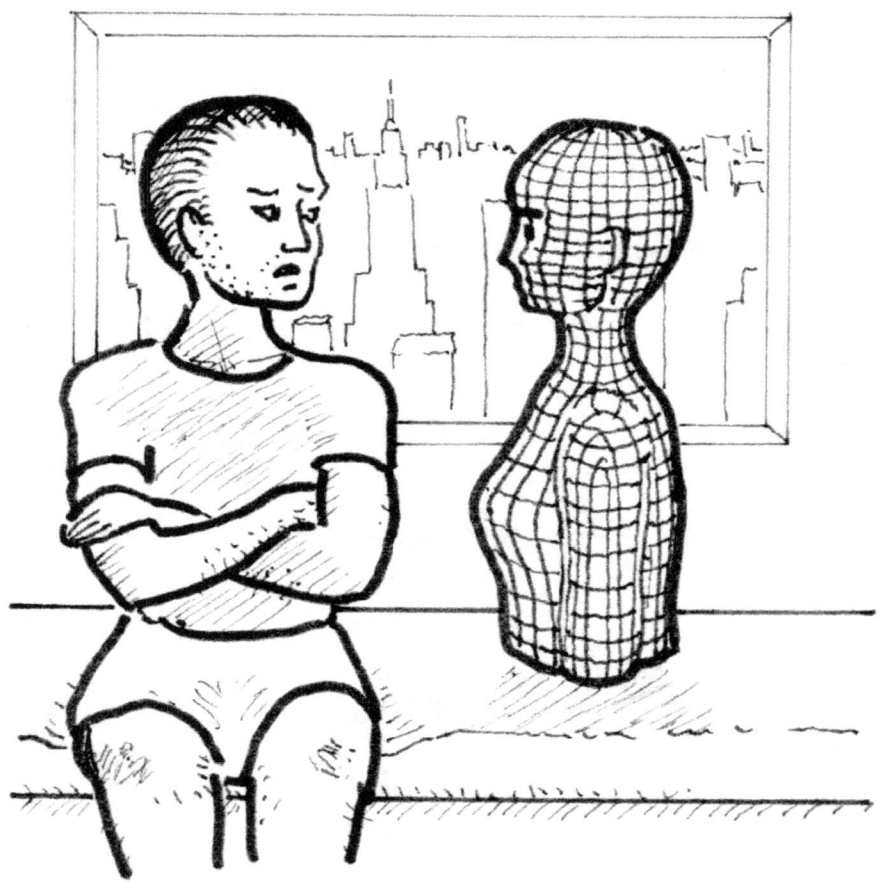

A blunt-spoken man of Manhattan
Had a girl-friend constructed of rattan.
He declared, to her face:
'You're a basket case, Grace:
This ain't goin' further than chattin'.'

Our sympathies lie with young Corder,
Whose mind was a froth of disorder:
　He'd proposed to Miss Dee,
　Who was keen as could be,
But realised he couldn't afford her.

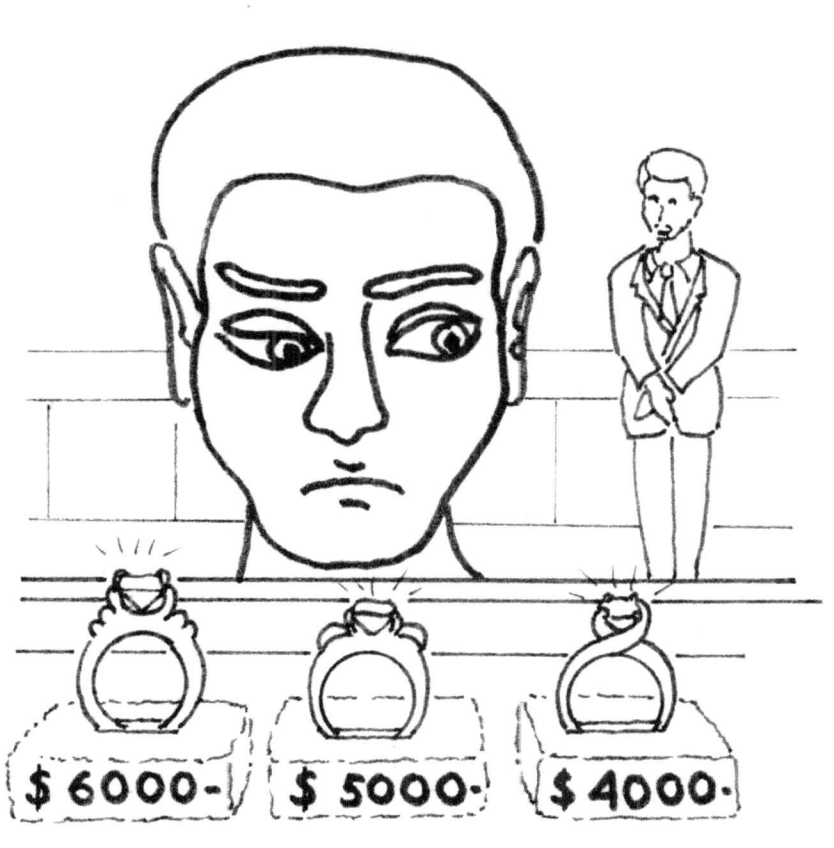

There was a young lass on page three
Whose figure was something to see:
Tom's eyes were impressed
With the size of her breast
To the point where they set themselves free.

A smooth-talking dandy called Mike
Once tried to make love on a bike
　The girl in this caper
　Disclosed to the paper
There was nothing about it to like!

Writing home from the outer Pacific,
A sailor claimed life was horrific.
He was trying to distract
From the evident fact
That the ladies out there were terrific.

Artistic Anomalies

An avant-garde dealer called Mallory
Once opened a modern art gallery.
The stuff he displayed!
Sadly, nobody paid,
So his taste had laid waste to a salary.

An eager young forger called Blake
Once knocked off a Constable fake.
A very good piece,
But he signed it 'Matisse',
Which was more than his dealer could take.

A tourist by name of Bernardo
Had followed a group round the Prado.
'There's pictures in there!'
He would later declare,
With a certain amount of bravado.

Greg Pastoll

An impressionist once tried to paint
Like a Cubist, with too much restraint.
The art cognoscenti
Raised eyebrows aplenty,
And one even fell in a faint.

There was an old geezer from Pisa
Who thought he was Julius Caesar:
 He posed for a painter
 Who rendered him quainter
Than Dali would do Mona Lisa.

'You think I can't paint like a Fauve?!'
Yelled a dauber. 'I'll show you, by Jove!'
He launched an attack,
Splashing orange and black,
But completely forgot to add mauve.

More without Pictures

There was a young lady in Nice,
Who thought she would join the police.
Her dad was appalled
As his bluff would be called
And he'd have to run business from Greece.

There was a young lady called Gloria
Who lived in the town of Pretoria.
When her husband, one day,
Said: 'We're moving away',
She could scarcely contain her euphoria.

An astronaut captain called Boone
Did ninety-nine laps of the moon.
That's a disciplined grind.
On return, he was fined
For driving his ship like a hoon.

A brainy young man of Mumbai
Was totally into AI.
His bot could predict
That his arse would be kicked
If he nicked some rupees on the sly.

A microwave techy called Green
Constructed a shaving machine.
If you switched the thing on,
Then your beard would be gone,
But so would your liver and spleen.

There was an accountant called Bligh
Who was nothing, if not very sly:
With a stroke of his pen
He had caused many men
To wave millions of dollars goodbye.

There was a young cretin called Spencer
Who, sadly, got denser and denser:
    Eventually he
    Was compelled to agree
That the time had arrived to join Mensa.

A learned professor of torsion
Would err on the safe side of caution.
    He never went out,
    Just in case he got gout.
Was he twisting things out of proportion?

While Jim went to study psychology,
Semantics, Old French and tribology,
    His brother earned riches
    By digging long ditches,
And never made any apology.

A devious banker called Claude
Was arrested on six counts of fraud.
When asked to explain:
'It wasn't for gain:
We do this because we are bored!'

A mathematician called Hector
Discovered a girl in his sector.
Her curves left his angle
Without any dangle:
He went asymptotic, and necked her.

A lady from Poland called Dottie
Had a crush on a prominent yachtie,
But marriage was out,
As this seagoing lout
Maintained a firm eye on his zloty.

A competent lady called Gwyneth,
Once captained a brig out of Plymouth.
　　When a sailor rebelled,
　　She emphatically yelled:
'Avast, there! I shouteth, you trimmeth!'

Parenting and children

There was a young baby from Ealing
Who spent all his afternoons squealing.
His mother said: " Jack,
I am taking him back!"
A most understandable feeling.

There was a young fellow called Berry,
Whose Christmas was not very merry.
He sat through old jokes
As re-told by his folks,
And, to top it, they offered him sherry.

There was a young toddler, in Pest,
Who flatly refused to get dressed.
He said that he would'a
If he'd lived in Buda,
But, in Pest, not so much as a vest.

A fussy old lady called Pat
Found a mouse made a house in her hat.
She screamed, and she ran,
But her grandson said: 'Gran,
You're lucky it wasn't a rat!'

On top of her table in Topham,
With carrots and pangas to chop 'em,
My aunt placed her twins,
And, with devilish grins,
They'd chop 'em, and nothing could stop 'em.

A very short rebel called Rocky
Refused to eat all of his gnocchi.
'You want to get tall?'
Said his mother, 'Eat all,
Or you're going to stay shrimpy and stocky!'

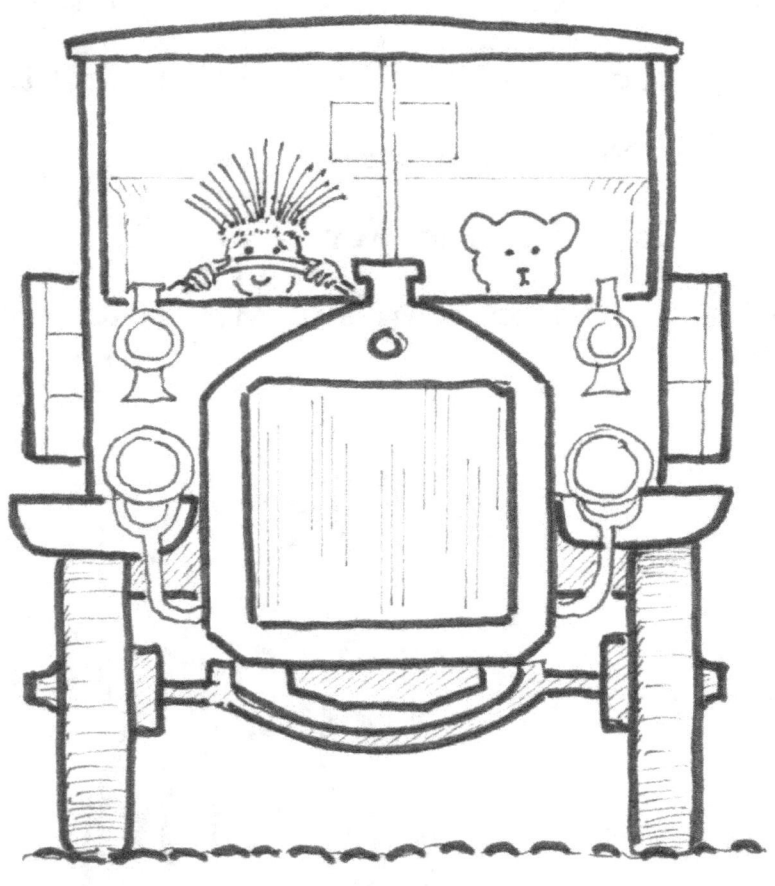

There was a young toddler called Dorrie,
Who really was quite a big worry.
She left her mom's flat
In a porcupine hat,
At the wheel of a forty-ton lorry.

A petulant teenager, Elfie
Was dragged by her parents to Delphi.
She hadn't a clue
What there was there to do,
So she busied herself with a selfie.

Greg Pastoll

A curious youngster from Truro
Once swallowed a Pound and a Euro.
The one made an exit,
The other a Brexit,
But, neither went back on the bureau.

An obstinate yob from Ascension
Had a minimum span of attention:
He would not read or write,
He refused to recite,
And declined to take part in declension.

A fiery young fellow called James
Enjoyed playing dressing-up games.
He roared down the street
In an outfit complete
As a dragon, but minus the flames.

There was a young dude with a rattle
Who found it a bit of a battle
To aim from his chair,
Pouring milk on her hair,
Without getting Sister to tattle.

The teacher observed that young Reggie
Was somewhat distracted and edgy.
He was not out of sorts,
But had worn the wrong shorts,
And was deeply involved in a wedgie.

A fussy young lady from Rye
Saw a fly come and land on her pie.
That gave her the willies:
She swapped it for Billy's
And wouldn't tell anyone why.

Young Simon O'Reilly (plus teddy)
Declared it was time to go steady.
His girl-friend, aged three,
Disinclined to agree,
Said: "Really, O'Reilly, already?'

There was a young toddler called Rose
Whose finger went right up her nose.
She pulled out a snollie
As big as her dolly,
And had to be cleaned with a hose.

A thrill-seeking scholar called Liam
Went off to the British Museum.
He'd heard it had things
Like the scrotums of kings,
And he made it his business to see 'em.

Sporting Shenanigans

A keen rugby player called Lumm
Was pushing like mad in the scrum,
But he fell out the back
From a whiff-waff attack
When his nose got too close to a bum.

A young tennis player called Hobbs,
Was an expert at hitting high lobs.
One ball went so high,
Her opponent said: 'Bye,
I'll be back when I've finished some jobs.'

An old golfing geezer called Dick
Scored two-thirty-three off the stick.
He got home at eight,
Which would seem rather late,
But his wife said: 'My God, that was quick!'

A sporting young fellow called Leach
Once raced a big croc up a beach.
Though he won by a metre,
The croc said: 'Hey, Peter,
A re-match: the score is one-each!'

An intrepid young lady called Coco
Once swam down the whole Orinoco.
  Back home in her state
  She was hailed as great,
But the locals just thought she was loco.

While exerting himself in the sports,
A fellow split open his shorts.
Now, a girl in the crowd
Whistled loud, so he bowed:
When his undies went too, there were snorts.

A karate exponent named Spence
Was called on to chop down a fence.
But, all of that mojo
He had at the dojo
Gave way to some good common sense.

A gymnast who'd murdered a man
Spent eighty-two years in the can.
By the time she got out,
She was too old to shout,
So she did a quick flick-flack, and ran.

A novice once leapt on a horse.
He lasted two seconds, of course.
For, harsh gravitation
Soon altered his station:
His teeth rattled something, in Morse.

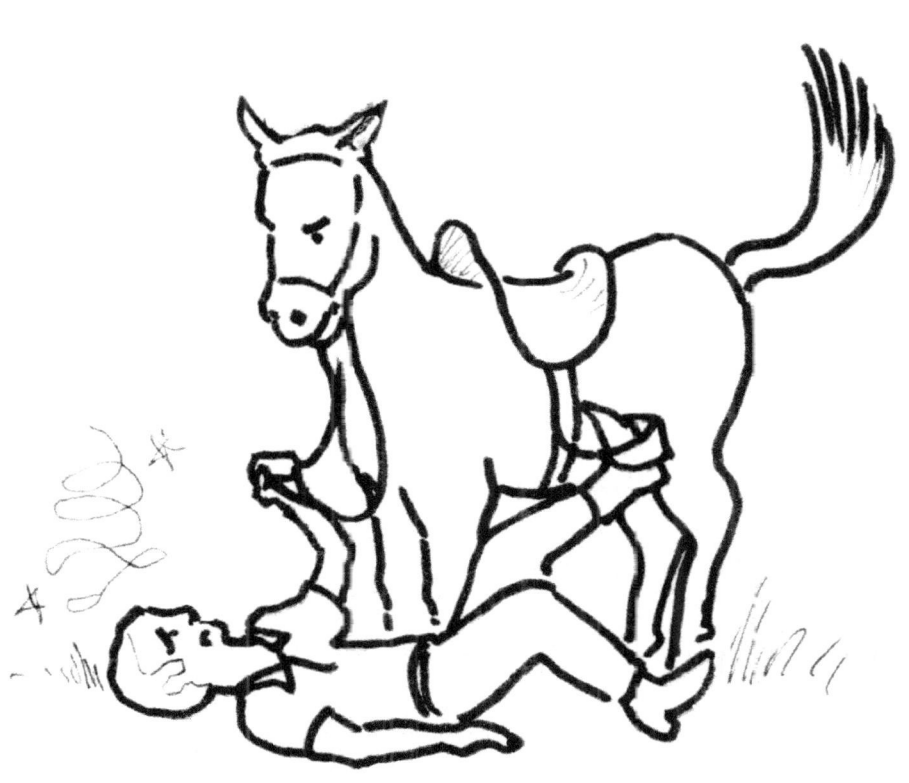

An archer let fly at a butt,
But a fly had just arched on his nut.
'That is not where I aimed!'
The poor fellow exclaimed.
'My eyes might as well have been shut!'

A very fast girl called Juanita
Declared she could outrun a cheetah.
This proved she could boast,
But, Juanita is toast,
As he said not a word, and still beat her.

A daredevil cyclist called Pike
Tried ramping the Rhine on his bike.
Then, halfway across,
His kid brother, Ross
Went whizzing past, fast, on his trike.

A young novice skier called Hope
Went down an impossible slope.
They found him in snow
At a hundred below,
But, is he still with us? Er...nope!

While boasting he'd swim the Zambezi,
A young man had set off all breezy.
But, seeing the crocs
And the hippos and rocks,
He suddenly turned rather queasy.

Pure Fantasy

An alien came down from space
To see what was up with this place.
He beamed a report,
Which amounted, in short,
To: 'Abort, they're a bloody disgrace!

A beast of the size of Godzilla
Demolished and ate someone's villa.
When they asked: 'How was that?'
He replied: 'Like a flat,
With slight undertones of vanilla.'

Have you heard of Ezekiel Drake
Whose neck was so long, it could break?
He wrapped it in plaster
To ward off disaster,
And combed his long hair with a rake.

A clever young man bought a poodle
For a very big bundle of boodle.
Was he mentally sound?
Yep: this marvellous hound
Could bake any pizza or strudel.

We met with man of poor taste
Whose nose-hairs hung down to his waist.
When he sneezed, they went mad,
'Holy crap!' shouted Dad,
And we ran off in desperate haste.

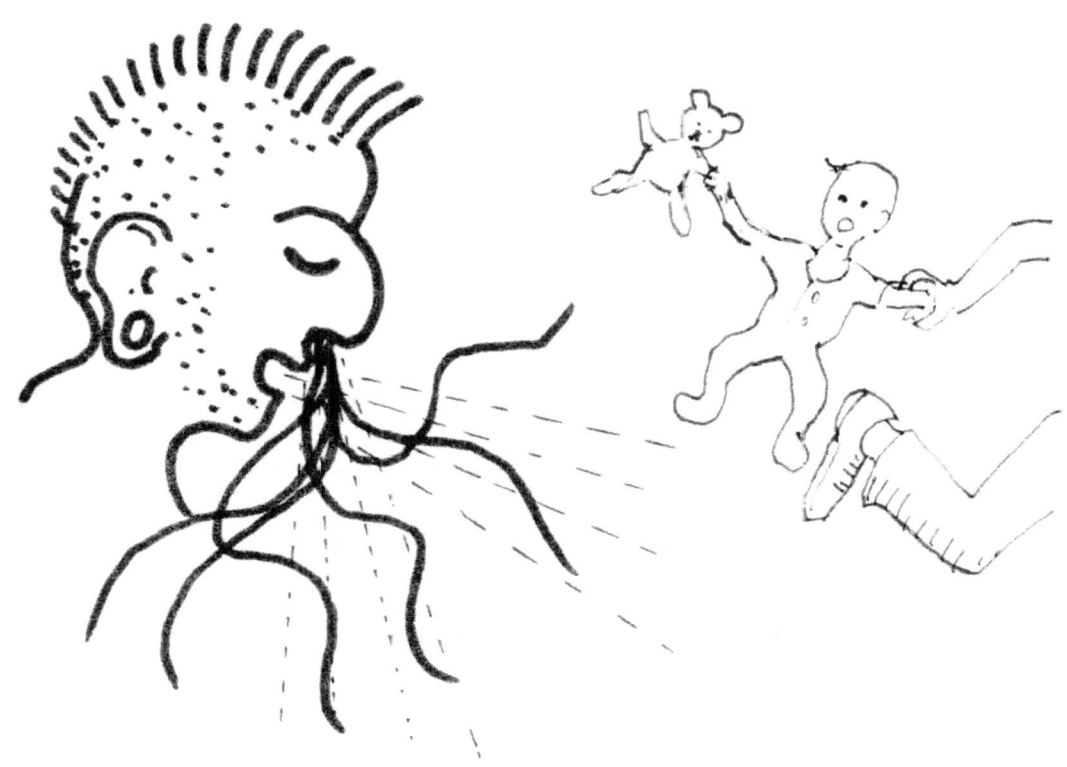

Greg Pastoll

As a great connoisseur of all beer,
Jerome had a very fine ear.
From the pop of the foam,
He could tell, could Jerome,
Who made it and what was the year.

There was a young fellow from Rex
Who was born with three heads and two necks.
To add to his woes,
He had only one nose,
So, he struggled a bit with his specs.

There was a young fellow in Wales
Who didn't like trimming his nails.
His coracle flew
Like a fly to a poo
When he held up his fingers for sails.

There's a town in the Arctic savannah
Where people eat nuts with a spanner.
They do not mind how
You engage with this chow,
But insist on a dignified manner.

Greg Pastoll

A dinosaur said to her hubby:
'Oh, Rex, you are getting so tubby.
You're your dad, to a T,
And like his, I can see
Those teeth that were sharp, are now stubby.

A sasquatch confides to a yeti:
'I really don't want to seem petty,
But I'm nervous as hell:
All those stories they tell
About humans: they make me go sweaty.'

Snippets from History

While being faced down by a giant,
A laddie once stood there, defiant:
He hauled out a sling:
Let me tell you, this thing
Was not 'health and safety' compliant.

A boy said to Richard Trevithick:
Could you please be a bit more specific?
This engine you moot:
Will it whistle and toot?
Adding smoke would be really terrific!

There was a young man of Gondwana,
Who slipped on an ancient banana,
He fell on his head,
And he later on said
He had caught a brief glimpse of Nirvana.

There was a young soldier from Thrace
Whose helmet was never in place.
A stone from a sling
Hit his temple: Ka-ping!
So he went back to base in a case.

A thoughtful old cave-man called Sonny
Came up with the concept of money.
His friends said 'Wha-dakka?
Ga-bidgee-na-kakka!
And tossed the poor bloke in the dunny.

Clothing Conundrums

An impudent fellow called Max
Once wore a false nose made of wax,
With warts and long hairs:
It scared off two bears,
Five crocs and a posse of yaks.

A maid from the district of Maas
Wore a dress as transparent as glass.
While it covered her well,
Any nitwit could tell
That she wasn't showing much class.

Young Jess thought to dress to impress,
By dolling herself to excess:
Her clothing got tighter
And louder, and brighter:
Jim noticed, but couldn't care less.

There was a young lady called Jenna
Who tried to fit in, in Vienna.
As far as we know,
It was all systems go,
As her hair was bright orange with henna.

Though Harold was horribly hairy,
He went to the ball as a fairy.
To make matters worse,
He arrived in a hearse,
Which was not only gross, it was scary!

A fastidious lass from Trieste
Was obsessed that her dress should stay pressed:
    When she joined the police,
      Any sign of a crease,
And she'd go out and make an arrest.

Have you heard about Shirley-Anne Hughes
Who chose to wear Lady-Luck shoes?
Those things were so high
That she felt she could fly,
Which she did, and she still has the bruise!

A notorious outlaw called Ned
With quite a large price on his head,
Came up with a helmet,
A wrap-around pelmet:
But that didn't help, as he's dead.

There was a young girl from the States,
Who used so much make-up on dates,
That, to lessen the chances
Of falling in dances,
She fitted her heels with weights.

I dated a dame from High Wycombe:
If she needed knickers, she'd nick 'em.
She was mostly tattoo,
And her hair was dyed blue:
My dad said: 'You sure can pick 'em!'

A penniless lady from Hocking
Once found she had only one stocking.
She bartered her dress
For another: I guess
The thought of just one was too shocking.

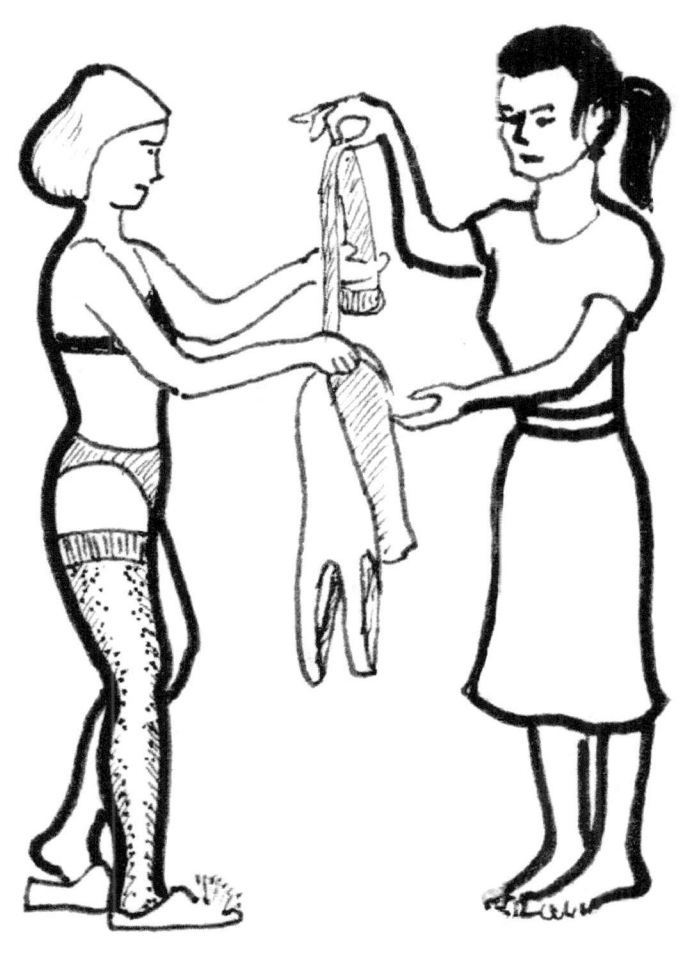

Greg Pastoll

A man from the island of Crete
Had two different sizes of feet.
You'd think he would lose
Every time he bought shoes,
But his twin brother helped out, a treat.

A girl in a fashion boutique
Saw a dress that was truly unique.
When she reached out to feel,
She let out a squeal:
It was on the proprietress, eek!

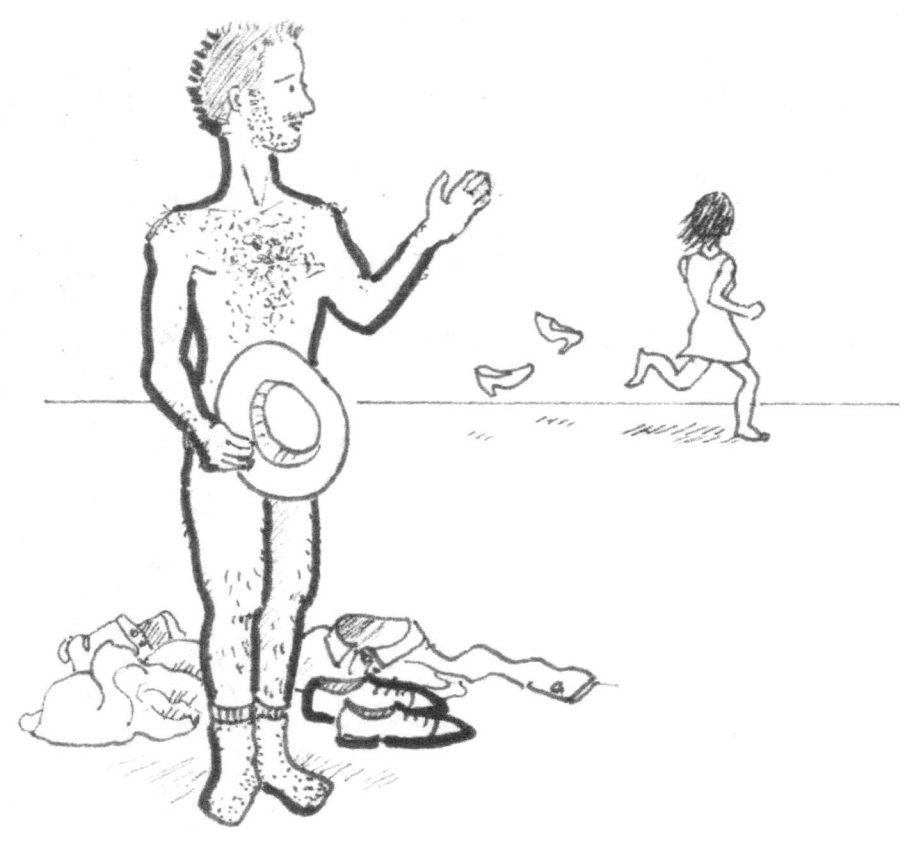

A fellow called Ratbag O'Grady
Once took off his hat to a lady.
Then he took off his suit
And his undies, to boot...
But she had vamoosed: he was shady.

There was a young lady from Weems,
Whose dress came apart at the seams.
A fellow said: 'Splendid:
Just stand still, I'll mend it.'
To which she replied: 'In your dreams!'

There was a young lad in Helsinki,
Whose favourite colour was pink: he
Had ordered online
What he thought was divine,
But his mother was shocked: it was kinky!

A fashion-wise lady from Queens,
Though really a person of means,
Got frostbitten knees
From a light autumn breeze,
On account of the holes in her jeans.

A tattooed young woman from Stroud
Wore clothing revealing and loud.
With unbridled passion
She went against fashion,
To be just like one of the crowd.

A fashion-blind girl called Babette
Once wore an enormous rosette.
It didn't look swell,
But it worked very well
At preventing her dress getting wet.

There was a young lady called Bella,
Whose hat had a purple propeller.
It didn't look grand
In the way she had planned,
But none of her friends dared to tell her.

An eccentric old gent, Mr Farrell
Was known for unusual apparel.
One day he appeared
In something less weird:
A pumpkin, two fish and a barrel.

Appendix

Suggestions for Writing your own Limericks

For those who enjoy the sound of rhyming verse, it can be fun to compose a limerick.

A limerick, as you will know by now, is a *very particular* form of short verse, consisting of five lines. It has a well-established rhythm, and a pattern of rhyming that goes AABBA. For example:

> A five-year old kid from Hong Kong
> Said 'Teddy-Bear's hair is too long':
> He picked up some shears,
> And, apart from the ears,
> He clipped it as smooth as a gong.

The importance of the rhyming pattern

Proper rhyming is vital to the elegance of a limerick. It simply is unforgivably crude to include near-rhymes such as time/fine, or bum/sun.

Near-rhymes sometimes work in song lyrics, because a song lyric will be strengthened by the musical accompaniment. In songs, near rhymes can even sometimes be quite clever and endearing. For example, in the film of the musical My Fair Lady, in the song 'On the street where you live', Freddie sings:

'…people stop and stare, they don't bother me/
for there's nowhere else on Earth that I would rather be…'

However, when you recite a limerick, it has no accompanying music to smooth over any minor flaws in its construction. It has to sound right on its own, because the sound pattern of a limerick *forms* its own music.

If the sound pattern (called 'scansion') works, it makes the limerick memorable.

In normal speech there are syllables that have emphasis and those that don't. This distribution of accents (strong and weak accents) is a firm characteristic of the way we speak in a particular language.

For instance, when you say 'Helsinki' in English, the strong accent is on the middle syllable. If you want to show it visually, you could write it as hel-SINK-i. It would make no sense to place the emphasis on the first or the last syllable of this word. Which means, if we use this word in a limerick, it has to fit into the accepted sound pattern of a limerick, and can only be used in certain positions.

If we denote the strong accents by the symbol '_' and the weak accents by the symbol '˘', then the sound pattern that is characteristic of most limericks goes as follows:

˘-˘˘-˘˘-   (There WAS an old MAN from al-SACE)
˘-˘˘-˘˘-   (Whose PLACE was a FLIPP-ing dis-GRACE)
˘-˘˘-   (He PICKED up a BROOM)
˘˘-˘˘-   (But he LOOKED round the ROOM)
˘-˘˘-˘˘-   (And PUT the thing BACK in its PLACE.)

This pattern of accents that is used in limericks is very traditional: sometimes it is acceptable to make minor deviations from it, although straying too far from this pattern could change the character of what you are writing so much as to render the result like an apologetic attempt at a limerick.

What to start with:

I have seldom started off a limerick with a story in mind that I want the limerick to convey. Most of the time (though not always) I start with an interesting proper noun that is suitable: either the name of a person or a place.

So, I write it down, and think of something preposterous that could happen, that ends in a word that rhymes with my first word.

For example: 'There was an old biddy called Hall.' Now what could happen to her, or what could she have done that sounds funny? Some possibilities:

Who went to a fancy-dress ball/ Who held up the bank in the mall/ Who made an emergency call/Who dated a dimwit called Paul/ Who lost her chemise in a squall/ Who was three and a half metres tall … Any one of these, or anything equally preposterous would do. The way it goes is up to your creativity.

Let's carry out the full process with another one: For example, you might start off with: **'There was a young lady from Cork…'**

The next step is to make a list of all the words you can think of that might rhyme with 'cork', such as:

fork, walk, talk, stalk, stork, dork, hawk, chalk, pork, gawk, York.

You would choose something to describe in the second line, that could lead to an interesting event. The more unusual, the better. Such as, for example:

Who took a giraffe for a walk/ Who combed her dog's hair with a fork/ Who made up her face using chalk/ Who got all her neighbours to gawk/ Who decided to paddle to York… and so on.

Now that you have set up the interesting event, with lines 1 and 2, you describe how it plays out, in lines 3, 4 and 5.

Line 3 often adds further drama to the situation, for example:

> **There was a young lady from Cork**
> **Who decided to paddle to York:**
> **When her boat sprang a leak….**

Now, line 4 will either add even more spice to the drama, or show what the character attempted to do, or describe how dire the situation is, to emphasise the difficulty of solving the predicament.

In this example, since we have used the word 'leak', we make a list of words that rhyme with 'leak', such as:

week, weak, freak, unique, beak, seek, creek, geek, cheek, meek, peak, speak, squeak, teak...

and we choose one of these, to see what happens. If it doesn't look as if the new line we have written is going to build up sufficient amusement in the story, we simply choose another word from our list, and rewrite line 4. Or, we rewrite line 3 and make up a new line 4 to match.

> **When her boat sprang a leak,**
> **She let out a shriek**

Usually, line 5 should present something of a surprise: a 'sting in the tail' of the storyline, or some unexpected consequence or unusual use of a word, or an anticlimax that is funny.

> **There was a young lady from Cork**
> **Who decided to paddle to York:**
> **When her boat sprang a leak,**
> **She let out a shriek,**
> **And jumped out, intending to walk.**

The hard part of composing a limerick is not to write line 5, but to write line 5 so that it is funny or intriguing.

Selecting suitable proper nouns, especially place names, to put at the end of line one:

You could start by naming some place-names and writing down all the words you can think of that rhyme with them, such as:

Rome: home, gnome, foam, comb, dome...

Ukraine: brain, train, main, stain, gain, again, inane, grain, lane, pain insane...

France: dance, enhance, prance, chance, lance, stance, advance...

Khartoum: room, broom, boom, doom, gloom, loom...

If you want to use one of these place names, the name has to be situated within the limerick in such a way as to fit into the traditionally accepted pattern of scansion.

Most place names have from one to four syllables.

If they have one syllable, no complications arise, and any place name will do, as long as other words can be found that rhyme with it:

There was a young doctor from Kent/Perth/ Guam/Troy/Seoul//Greece/Crete/Chad…

If the place name has two syllables, the word should preferably have the accent on the *second* syllable, not the first, or else the scansion will be wrong.

You could have, for example:

'There was a young man of Dubai/Dunkirk/The Hague/The Cape/L.A./Pusan/New York/Mumbai/Japan/Quebec…'

It would break the scansion pattern completely if you used the place name 'London', or 'Joburg' or 'Phoenix' or 'Sydney' at the end of line 1.

You can get around this by inserting the place name at some other position in the line, not at the end of the line, such as: 'In London, in sixteen-oh-three…' but this is a further refinement altogether.

One can *sometimes* use a two-syllable place name with the accent on the first syllable, provided other words can be found to rhyme with it, for example:

There was an old farmer in China

Who went to a water-diviner…

If the place-name has three syllables, and is to be used at the end of line 1, the accent should be on the *second* syllable: for example

There was an old man of Djibouti/Karachi/Kentucky/Angola/Toronto…

but not on the first syllable: these don't work: Carletonville/Hollywood/ Mozambique//Manchester/Tuscany…

If you intend to use a three-syllable name, then it might fit in better at some place other than the end of line 1. For instance, you could have line 1 read: ' A Hollywood actress of note…' or 'In Tuscany once was a prince…'

A place name with four or more syllables is way too long and will be difficult, if not impossible, to fit into a limerick. (Such as Johannesburg/ Valparaiso/Vereeniging/Edinburgh/Thessaloniki…)

Using personal names at the end of line one:

The same guidelines that apply to place names apply to names of persons that one might use in the first line:

One syllable: any name will work, for instance Mark, Wright, Green, Jones, May, John, Jen, Joy… as long as other words can be found that rhyme with it.

Two syllables: emphasis on the second syllable makes it easier to achieve good scansion, if you plan to use single-syllable words at the end of lines 2 and 5, for example:

Elaine (brain, cane, Dane, gain, grain, main…) and Yvonne (con, gone, on)…

Many two-syllable names in English have the emphasis on the *first* syllable, and these will also work, provided that you can find other words that rhyme with them, that also have the same emphasis:

Millie (silly, frilly, dilly) Peter (eater, cheetah, fleeter) Adam (madam, had 'em) Basil (frazzle, dazzle) Bridget (fidget, midget) Jerry (merry, ferry) Ellen (melon, felon) Hector (inspector, detector) Dutton (button, mutton)…

Using personal names with three syllables: these are harder to fit into a limerick, but occasionally can work, e.g. Michaela (paler, derail her, whaler, sailor).

It is often not easy to get all the features you want in a limerick to work together. If this happens, it may help to put it way and look at it again with a couple of days' break, or even a few weeks. Then you see it with fresh eyes, and are not so attached to the line of thought with which you began.

Ask anyone who worked hard to get a limerick to succeed: they will tell you it was worth the effort.

....

About the Author

Gregory Pastoll engages in many different creative endeavours. Writing humorous verse is only one of his hobbies.

Concerning the quirkiness of these limericks: Greg has always tried to see the funny side of situations, looked at them from unusual viewpoints, and maintained the right to see the world as it appears to him, not as others would have one see it. He thinks creativity has something to do with being uninhibited, so that seemingly crazy ideas that come to you are not filtered out before their usefulness has been explored.

About the drawings: Greg has enjoyed drawing and painting since he was three years old, and has picked up what he knows by observation, trial and error, and by devoting time and energy to it.

Other creative writing by this author

Greg has published in book form two collections of stories in rhyming verse. One for people aged 10 and up: 'The King of Kafooni and other rhyming tales' (2008), illustrated by Rudolf Joubert, and one for adults: 'The Hippopotamologist and other quirky stories in rhyme' (2013), not illustrated. See short extracts from these further down.

A further collection of his rhyming stories (for ages 8 to 12) has been recorded in the form of a CD: 'Riveting Rhymes', and likewise a prose story of his for children aged 3 to 10 'The Bright Blue Frog'.

He has written original scripts and lyrics for five musicals for young people, two of which have been performed in a primary school in Cape Town: These were: 'The Pirate Queen' (2007), which bears no relation whatsoever to two other musicals of the same name, and 'Jovano's Question' (2009). The music for both of these was composed by Anthea Parnell, and both were directed by Jacqueline Pienaar. Another of his musical scripts for young people, though not yet performed, has been published as a book: 'A Whale in Paris' (2014).

Other creative accomplishments

Greg learned the craft of violin-making under the tutelage of Brian Lisus and completed three violins, two of which were sold to competent young players.

He has designed and built wooden furniture for his family's own use, project-managed the building of two houses, and designed board games, one of which, 'The Cricket Game', was manufactured and sold in the 1990s, endorsed by Bob Woolmer, who formerly played cricket for England, and who was at the time the coach of the South African cricket team.

He has been painting landscapes, portraits and geometrical abstracts as a major activity for many years, alongside his formal work life as a lecturer.

Greg's paintings may be seen on two websites: redbubble.com and ozartfinder.com.

Formal writings

His formal career spanned several teaching appointments: as a lecturer in Mechanical Engineering (Cape Technikon and Cape Peninsula University of Technology), a senior lecturer in Teaching Methods in Higher Education (University of Cape Town), and spells of teaching English as a foreign language in South Korea and in Austria.

In 2019 Greg published a series of three volumes entitled 'Basic Engineering Mechanics Explained', which is a guide for first and second-year engineering students, based on his experiences of devising and refining his own teaching material when lecturing. This series he illustrated himself.

He has also published two books on education: 'Motivating People to Learn… and teachers to teach' (2002), and 'Tutorials That Work' (1992).

Greg lives with his wife in Perth, Western Australia.

Extracts from other published rhyming stories by this author

From 'On The Blink' in 'The Hippopotamologist and other quirky stories in rhyme' *(for all ages, but mostly of interest to mature people)*

> Mrs Mildred Moxton-Mink
> Hurled some dishes in the sink,
> Whacked the dog, and kicked the cat,
> Then bolted on her Sunday hat.
>
> She slammed the door, and off she went,
> To go and get her arm re-bent.
> Such *rudeness!* Oh, it makes me *sick!*
> But then, she *was* a robot chick.
>
> Her husband called her Mildred, see,
> But sometimes Sue or Jenna-Lee.
> Her real name was 4-3-2
> Type BJ 40, blonde and blue- ...

From 'Mike's Hotel' in 'The King of Kafooni and other rhyming tales' *(ages 10 and up)*

> 'I'm not impressed!' the parting guest
> Declared at Mike's Hotel.
> 'My bedroom rug was mostly bug,
> My pillow had a smell!'
>
> 'I couldn't close the window-blind:
> It flapped all night, and squeaked.
> I had to wear my Wellingtons
> Because the toilet leaked!'

'I rang the bell for service, once,
Was forced to wait an hour,
And, when she came, the service dame
Threw up inside the shower!' ...

From 'Beetle Ka-Teetle' recorded in 'Riveting Rhymes' *(ages 8 to 12)*

Beetle Ka-Teetle said Boodleroy Bug
Should really come look at the hole he had dug.
'Nah! What is so special about an old hole?'
Said Boodleroy Bug, from the top of his pole.

'Come check this,' said Beetle. 'It's deep and it's wide:
It makes a good place for a beetle to hide.'
'Well, hide, then, you nitwit. I hope you have fun,
But *I* shall be staying to tan in the sun.'

He spread out his lilo, and hummed like a top,
Then rubbed all his legs with some sun-tanning glop.
'Say, Beetle!' he shouted. 'Come out of that nook,
And tell me how *cool* these new shades of mine look!' ...

. . . .

www.ingramcontent.com/pod-product-compliance
Lightning Source LLC
Chambersburg PA
CBHW060532010526
44107CB00059B/2620